Praise fo
Everything I Needed
I Learned from My S

"*Everything I Needed to Know I Learned From My Six-Month-Old* is the perfect companion for any new mother. I wish I had had this book ten years ago when my first daughter was born—I would have felt so much less alone. Kuwana Haulsey's voice is full of humor and grace, but what I love most about her is that she tells it like it is. Reading this book is like chatting with a close friend."

—Kate Hopper,
author of *Use Your Words: A Writing Guide for Mothers*

"Baby as meditation—that's the idea that award-winning novelist Haulsey came up with after the birth of her son. Caught up in the overwhelming, full-time spiral of loving and caregiving-on-demand, she suddenly realized that her infant son was also a spiritual master, pure in his existence in the world, dealing with everything he experienced with a wide-open heart and mind. She decided to learn from his example. Mindfulness practice tells us to stay in the present and face our truth. Mothering an infant requires just that. Haulsey began to work with the experience, letting it take her into life review, self-realization, and, eventually, gratitude. It's especially valuable for first-time mothers. Even those who aren't parents will be inspired by the honesty of this life-affirming, real-world book."

—*Retailing Insight*

"With the talent of a master artist, Kuwana Haulsey paints a picture of the true blessings of being a parent. She transports you from day-to-day parenting rituals to a place that gently and quietly reminds you to be in that very special and precious parenting moment—for it is a moment that is fleeting. The warmth of your baby's skin, the first giggle, the beginnings of the emergence and continual evolution of a personality that is uniquely theirs...this is indeed what it is to be in the presence of a miracle. How lucky we are to have Kuwana Haulsey to take us to that place and space in time that every parent relishes and treasures."

—Carole Brody Fleet,
author of *Happily Even After*

everything
i needed to
know i learned
from my
six-month-old

everything i needed to know i learned from my six-month-old

AWAKENING TO UNCONDITIONAL SELF-LOVE IN MOTHERHOOD

KUWANA HAULSEY

FOREWORD BY MICHAEL BERNARD BECKWITH

Viva
EDITIONS

Published in the United States by Viva Editions,
an imprint of Cleis Press, Inc.,
2246 Sixth Street, Berkeley, California 94710.

Printed in the United States.
Cover design: Scott Idleman/Blink
Cover photograph: mark hooper/Getty Images
Text design: Frank Wiedemann
First Edition.
10 9 8 7 6 5 4 3 2 1

Trade paper ISBN: 978-1-936740-53-6
E-book ISBN: 978-1-936740-62-8

Library of Congress Cataloging-in-Publication Data

Haulsey, Kuwana, 1973-
  Everything I needed to know I learned from my six-month-old : awaken-ing to unconditional self-love in motherhood / by Kuwana Haulsey. -- First edition.
       pages cm
  ISBN 978-1-936740-53-6 (alk. paper)
  1. Haulsey, Kuwana, 1973- 2. Authors, American--21st century--Family relationships. 3. Mother and infant. 4. Motherhood. I. Title.
  PS3558.A7576Z46 2013
  818'.603--dc23
                                    2013026581

Angels, like parables and fine poetry, speak in many layers of meaning and mystery, trying to express the inexpressible. If we ignore them, our lives are the poorer.

—BISHOP DESMOND TUTU

For Kingston, my angel,
and for Jackson, the littlest angel
with the shiny new wings

Contents

Your children are not your children. They are the sons and daughters of life's longing for itself. They come through you, but not from you. And though they are with you, yet they belong not to you. You may house their bodies, but not their souls. You may strive to be like them, but seek not to make them like you. You are the bows from which your children as living arrows are sent forth. The Archer sees the mark upon the path of the infinite, and He bends you with His might that His arrows may go swift and far. Let your bending in the archer's hand be for gladness; for even as He loves the arrow that flies, so He loves also the bow that is stable.

—KHALIL GIBRAN

Foreword

THERE ARE PRECIOUS MOMENTS IN LIFE, MOMENTS OF incredible rarity and beauty during which we become immersed in the present without anxiety about the future. There's no concern over things that may have happened in the past or worry about how life might turn out because we're conscious that life is perfect just as it is. Children effortlessly provide us with these reminders of the inherent goodness of life; with just a smile, a laugh, or a hug from a beloved child, we are instantly brought to a place of timeless, joyous connection wherein nothing else seems to exist.

Years ago when my daughter Micaela was an infant, I had the opportunity to stay home and be her primary caregiver. I look back on that time as a very precious and wonderful turning point in my life. I remember how I didn't like changing diapers, so I gave her a bath every time she went to the bathroom. People often commented on how I kept my baby so immaculately clean, but they never knew my true motives. During those days I learned firsthand how children have the capacity to keep us connected to the present moment, one that is filled with love, beauty, and total connection.

As a consciously committed caregiver, you learn that there isn't anything you wouldn't sacrifice for another human being. The boundaries between yourself and the other disappear; you would literally give your life for someone else. The strength of this kind of bond quietly begins to erode any sense of selfishness or separation.

As the years go by these bonds cement and expand. Today, more than thirty years later, my bond with my daughter—the love and vulnerability in that relationship—has only deepened. It would not surprise me if this legacy of devotion first emerged in another dimension of time and space, but as a parent I have a direct experience of it here and now, in this lifetime. Equally as important, my interactions with my children (and now my grandchildren) allowed me to become aware of gifts, strengths, and capacities within myself that were birthed along with them. My growth through fatherhood taught me to hold a space of compassion and unconditional love for myself, which in turn allowed me to model these qualities to my children as they went through the challenges of growing up—especially through their teen years. It made me a better role model for them.

It is often taught in African cosmology that children and elders are closer to the other world than those who are middle-aged. Children come freshly from the realm of no-time-space and elders are closer to returning into no-time. Our interactions with our children provide the means for us to continually return to that which is real, eternal, and vital. These are the graces I received throughout the years of caretaking my precious daughter, graces that are essential to my spiritual and emotional development. It humbles me to realize that I was learning as much from her as she was learning from me.

Children don't arrive in this world as blank slates to be written upon, even though the popular belief is that they do. They come to us imbued with proclivities, insights, and gifts—qualities that they've already developed in the course of their soul's existence. If we watch and listen we can glean what they have come to share with the world. When we as parents understand this, we become aware of their power to impact our own lives for the better. We come to regard them as gift bearers offering us the opportunity to delve deeply into the sacredness of mothering and fathering.

In our fast-paced society success is commonly measured by one's profession or credentials and the material gains these garner, rather than by one's character and contributions to life. In this atmosphere it is easy to overlook the sacred aspects of parenthood. When outer validation from others becomes of paramount importance, our spiritual and emotional connections to one another become devalued.

But the joy that arises through an authentic connection between a child and a loving caregiver is incomparable. You feel it the moment you come face-to-face with the utter vulnerability of a newborn. And you protect it with your very life. You feel it when a baby opens his or her heart to you and you reciprocate this unconditional love. The joy overflows when you watch a child take a first step, speak that first word, and begin to express their unique personality. The sacred art of parenting is something to be savored, not rushed through. Learning to surrender yourself to the moment, no matter what it looks like, and to find the beauty in it is a gift that will serve you throughout your lifetime.

From that perspective every task can be used as an avenue for awakening to who and what we are, to our own essential nature, which contains the innocence of a child. Dealing with an infant who depends upon you for their survival requires being present and focused. That requirement of sustained attention, when applied consciously, develops attentiveness and intentionality, the very foundation of spiritual practice and inner transformation. Being clear about your intentions is very important: Why do you wake up every day? What is your motivation? What is your cause for taking action? Honing your attention means consciously asking yourself where you are placing your focus on a moment-by-moment basis.

When you have a baby, your attention and awareness must be fully present; if not, it takes only seconds for tragedy to take place. With the intention to be a vehicle of love, education, inspiration—a place of safety and security for your child—it becomes vital to practice what we might call an open-eyed meditation. A parent or caregiver who commits to such an endeavor will learn profound lessons and give their child great gifts.

To welcome a baby into a family instantly puts you through the crucible of transformation. On some days it definitely feels daunting or overwhelming. It may seem as though life would be much easier without all that responsibility. You may fantasize about driving the Pacific Coast Highway and looking out at the ocean, doing whatever you want and feeling free. But raising a child with intention and consciousness makes you a candidate for insights that can ultimately lead to true freedom, which is a spiritual practice that supports you in evolving into your greatest self.

This idea is the basis for this book. I've known Kuwana Haulsey for many years. I've loved her work as a novelist. In her previous books, *The Red Moon* and *Angel of Harlem*, she used fictional stories to convey the essence of sacred truths. But in *Everything I Know*, she brings to us something from her personal life, from the depths of her intimate discoveries as a mother seeking to grow into her own authentic power and wisdom so that she might inspire the same in her child. Kuwana's lessons and insights shared in this book are all based on hard-won, firsthand experience.

These pages are filled with moments of wonder, joy, heartbreak, and revelation that will resonate with anyone who has ever loved a child. Kuwana's perspective is refreshing, particularly at a time when many voices in our society proclaim distaste for the responsibilities and burdens of parenting. This book is a refresher course, a reminder of the blessings of parenthood and that the sacrifices one willingly makes in raising a child are ultimately meant to enrich one's life, not impoverish it. In fact, the etymology of the word *sacrifice* is from the Latin *sacer*, which means sacred, holy, consecrated.

In *Everything I Know*, Kuwana Haulsey speaks to the spiritual unfolding that occurs when we take on the sacred responsibility to love, protect, and guide our children; in turn they birth within us a greater embodiment of unconditional love. An incomparable storyteller, Kuwana allows us to see our own stories embedded within her personal tale. The wisdom, humor, and love she so wholly expresses will encourage us all to cherish the blessing and practice of sacred parenting.

Michael Bernard Beckwith

Introduction

MY SON PLAYS WITH ANGELS ON A REGULAR BASIS.

One particular day, he lay draped over my arm, reaching out for a hand I couldn't see, smiling and laughing. His little nose wrinkled and I imagined the feathery tip of a wing gliding in front of his face. Then he burst into an ecstatic squeal and plopped his head down against my chest, hiding his face from the other realms.

What a magnificent being, I thought. Of course I was referring to my baby, not the angel I imagined perched on the end of my bed. As Kingston laughed, I marveled at how thin the veil between heaven and earth can be when you're only six months old.

Slowly, my son brought his attention back down into the room. I held him close, gently bouncing him up and down, until he began to drift to sleep. When his eyes finally closed I laid him in the middle of our bed and just stared, tracing the lines of his body over and over again with my eyes. He was soft and pillowy, full of curves and folds and dimples. My son sighed in his sleep and pursed his tiny lips, looking altogether perfect, so much like God-in-the-flesh that it took my breath away.

I couldn't help but wonder, what in the world is he doing here with *me*? How did I get so lucky?

Of course, the reality is that luck has nothing to do with it. Parenting, I quickly learned, is all about choices. There are good choices and not-as-good choices—and we all make them. The more time I spent nurturing my son, the more he inspired me to examine the soundness of all my choices. Prodded by his tiny fingers, I began to reevaluate my life with a level of honesty that had eluded me in the past.

It felt like he'd reached inside my mind and flicked on the light. Suddenly, I was able to see a whole slew of secret thoughts and beliefs that had dictated the way I'd made my decisions up to that point; my choices created predictable results that kept showing up as the unintended consequences and circumstances of my life. I became uncomfortably aware of patterns that I'd been unable to break: the places in my relationships where "good enough" had become good enough, the dreams that had started to seem far-fetched, the excuses that I'd grown far too comfortable believing and repeating. I also noticed how quickly the critic in the back of my mind would pounce on any opportunity to berate these supposed shortcomings.

It dawned on me that I would never, *ever* criticize or judge Kingston by the same stingy measures. A mother knows that her child is precious and beautiful, worthy of unconditional love simply because he or she exists. No matter how imperfect it may seem at any given moment, a mother's love is rich, deep, and unending. Babies deserve no less.

When and how, I wondered, did I start accepting less for myself?

More importantly, how could I learn to give myself the same kind of unconditional love that so easily flowed from me to my child? Could I soothe, nurture, support, and celebrate myself the way I did him? If I tripped and fell over a hole in my thinking, instead of spending a day or a week wondering why in the world I hadn't seen that shortfall coming, could I simply pick myself up, clean myself off, and head back out to play?

Without a doubt, my ability to be a conscious participant in my own spiritual, mental, and emotional expansion was crucial to my ability to guide my son to his highest potential. After all, where we come from has so much to do with where we go. And where we go in life is dictated, ultimately, by who we are. Herein lies the premise at the heart of this book: who we are—our values, passions, joys, sorrows, and creative impulses—is, in the final analysis, the set of traits our children learn to mirror in their own ways. "Do as I say" becomes "Do as I do," which hopefully evolves into "Be as I am."

When we love ourselves unconditionally, we show our children what it looks like and feels like to live comfortably in the heart of God. As we make a conscious practice of standing in unconditional love, our lives become more vibrant and audacious, full of power and meaning. It becomes possible to chart exciting new courses in our own development, even as we shoulder the incredible responsibility of being the ballast that keeps everyone else sailing smoothly forward.

Of course, all this sounds really good on paper. In reality, it's much too easy to get lost in the constant demands of motherhood. Oftentimes, the open-ended desires of the heart quietly start to fade—so deep is a mother's love that sometimes you barely miss them until they're gone. If someone had told pre-pregnant Kuwana that it would be so easy to let my *self* get totally overshadowed by my child's needs, I would've called them crazy. In fact, I did call them crazy. Friend after friend patted my belly and warned, *You just wait! It'll be all about the baby as soon as he gets here. You'll see!* Of course, I ignored them.

Then the baby came.

As the weeks and months raced by, I had the all-too-familiar realization that if I wasn't vigilant, my lifelong dreams could become permanently eclipsed by the realities and responsibilities of this new life. Slowly, I started losing sight of the real *me*—the me of spiritual inquiry, of questing and journeying, of introspection, vision, challenge, and change. The many things that needed to be done on a daily basis loomed much larger in my mind than the things I had always wanted to do. I was finding my way, and losing it, at the same time. But, of course, seeing the problem and knowing what to do about it are two completely different things.

Then, while watching my son sleep that afternoon, it hit me. *Be as a little child...*

The key to a deeper understanding of all my questions was lying right in front of my eyes. Literally. Babies, I realized, are tiny little masters of the universe, manifesters of the highest order. The consciousness of a child is like a pristine river winding its way toward its destination The water doesn't hold the reflection of the tree it just passed along its shore, calling it wonderful or ugly. It doesn't fight against the rocks that have fallen down and obstructed its way. It simply charts a new path and stays in the flow. Children are the same way (before they're domesticated, to use the term of Don Miguel Ruiz). Joy or loneliness, comfort or pain, fear or love—each sensation has its place in the moment, then it's gone. The baby remains completely available, sure of itself with its arms open wide to life.

Enlightenment, it occurred to me, is the warm, soft glow that radiates from a child's heart.

I was able to see what awakened consciousness looked like by watching a six-month-old boy, because he'd never been to sleep (figuratively, of course, though sometimes it felt pretty literal). As an adult I wondered if I could learn—or relearn—to be like that. I believed that I could. Kingston was teaching me how. As I raised my son, I discovered that he was also raising me.

His presence, so delightful and adoring, encouraged me to explore motherhood as a means of waking up, a pathway to discovering the hidden wealth of my soul. Rather than leading me away from myself, motherhood has the power to lead me toward full freedom of expression. My son's touch brought water to the dry places, inviting me to drench myself in the same unconditional love that I shower him with every day.

Hopefully this book will encourage you to do the same.

Finding the Courage to Emerge

Dare you have the courage to be who you really are?

—PIR VILAYAT

THE GIRL ACROSS THE ROOM RAISED HER HEAD AND THE
look in her eyes stopped my breath.

Who is this? I wondered. My God.

She was beautiful, with long heavy braids hanging down
the middle of her back, golden skin, and uncertain eyes. People
don't like to be stared at when they're frightened, so I looked
away to give her some privacy. A minute later she hunched
her back and moaned, once more immersed in what was happening to her body, this process of becoming something new.
I wanted to tell her that everything would be OK, but I wasn't
sure that it would be. It was hours until dawn and she was
already naked and sweating, pacing heavily around the room.
This poor girl was about to have the longest day of her life.

As I watched her transform in the mirror in front of me, a
story I'd read weeks before flashed through my mind.

It seems that there's a tribe in Africa where, the first time
a woman leaves home following the confinement period after
giving birth, everyone she meets along the road greets her
with a sacred song otherwise reserved for warriors returning
from battle. She's honored as having lived through a rite of
passage that will forever mark her womanhood as abundant
and powerful and blessed. She's respected as a fully franchised

member of the most ubiquitous and yet most extraordinary group of beings in our collective experience: mothers.

There was something about this vision of strength and power—and the recognition of worth that went along with it—that appealed to me. This archetype of divine motherhood walking alone along the dusty roadside in my mind's eye was someone whose wisdom was innate and whose voice was unmistakable. Her words mattered, so she used them with clarity and purpose. She gave to those around her from the overflow of her spirit, not from the dregs. She had a sensual, arresting beauty all her own; she released the pressure to look like or act like anyone other than herself. The temptation to try to be "perfect" or "have it all together" for anyone else's benefit wouldn't even be a temptation for her. She would know how much richer life was on the other side of that lure, where failure might be an option, but living in fear and pretense was not.

The desire to know (and be loved by) this divine mother is intimately familiar. Yet somehow she seems so far removed. This is the mother we all *think* that we have before we get grown and start nitpicking at the humanity of the women we were born to. This is the woman we secretly want to be, even though it very often seems like she doesn't exist. But she does exist. I know. I've seen her. She's been there, no matter how big or small her part, in the face of every pregnant woman and mother I've ever seen look deeply at a child with love.

I wanted her face to be my face too. I wanted to allow this

woman of purpose, this woman I'd always believed myself to be inside, to emerge from the girl in the mirror. But how? Babies know how to be birthed. Mothers do not always know how to birth themselves.

I'd pondered these thoughts for weeks, though not in a serious way. I just loved the idea of being able to magically summon my inner warrior to carry me through the end of pregnancy. As fantasies go, it was really quite enthralling. My body had gotten so enormously awkward that I was barely able to roll out of bed by myself. Under the circumstances, it seemed only fair and fitting that there'd be a trade-off of some kind. Maybe I'd given up gracefulness and freedom and the ability to see my feet, but in return I would gain access to a mysterious new power within me. This power was destined to rise up and, at just the right moment, give me the strength to conquer any challenge.

There was something potent within me waiting to be birthed right alongside the baby curled up in my body. Just like the women in the little African village, I'd summon my warrior and she would kneel down before me without protest, generously offering up her services as midwife, ready to birth me into my new purpose, and a higher level of consciousness. It sounded wonderful.

However, as another contraction began to swell, I started having some doubts. The face in the mirror lost its subtle glow and turned back into my own familiar, sweating, scrunched-up, agonized face. Struggling to breathe through the panic,

I wondered if maybe I'd made a really big miscalculation. It was seriously looking like the warrior goddess I'd been counting on would be a no-show.

As a self-described pacifist (read: people pleaser), I may have seemed unworthy to her. But without her how would I get through this, the birth of my first child? I wanted my son more than I wanted my next breath, but how *exactly* was I supposed to get him here? This only sounds like a simple question if you've never been in labor before. What had I gotten myself into? Was I honestly prepared to become a mother?

The short answer is: of course not. But you couldn't have told me that at the time. In my mind, before the contractions started, I had it all together. In reality, what I had was a pretty crib, some woefully unimaginative pregnancy books, a closet full of tiny clothes, and the incredible assumption that somehow these things equipped me to be a mother. It was pretty audacious thinking. But in my own defense, there was no way that I could possibly have known what was about to happen.

Going through childbirth for the first time is a lot like going cliff diving when you can't swim very well. Boldly you jump, trusting the exhilaration of the moment to carry you through. If it does, great. If it doesn't, well, its not like you can turn back. When that first contraction hits, you are airborne. Your entire being is alight with the profound and shocking realization of the true meaning of the word commitment. In my pre-pregnancy life, I could barely commit to a morning yoga class. Yet here I was, asking myself, and my husband, to commit to the most profound change that two human beings can undergo. And what about the baby? I'd heard it said by spiritual types who supposedly know these things that between birth and death, birth is the more appalling of the two experiences. How would the baby get through all of this?

As the contraction receded, I kneeled down and ran my hand over the huge mound of my belly. I whispered words that I hoped were comforting, looking for some sign that our son felt my presence and was consoled. But there was no 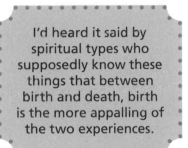 movement, nothing at all. My heart jumped. I tapped on my stomach a few times. *Hello in there?* Nothing. I pushed down on my belly, harder than I intended to, trying to get him to move. Annoyed, Kingston pushed back and flipped over on his side. If he could've used the placenta as a cover to throw over his head, he would have. That boy was fast asleep in there and clearly letting me know: *Go away, Mama! Cut it out!*

Even in the middle of labor, he was cutting up.

Kingston was nothing if not consistent. Before our son was even born, he was a talker, a doer, a whirlwind of quick opinions. He'd constantly sent messages to me from the womb, tapping out clear demands like Morse code across the skin at the base of my belly. *Mama, it's time to eat!* If I ignored him, or didn't move fast enough toward the refrigerator, he would waft down and plop onto my bladder, crushing it like a stress ball. As soon as I put something, anything, in my mouth, he'd say a polite thanks by floating up and away, happily going about his pre-birth business.

Oftentimes, I'd found myself wondering what would happen if I were more like my son. What kinds of things might I say if I hadn't learned, at some point in my life, that being polite had a greater resale value than being honest? Kingston, on the other hand, had no such qualms. He was relentlessly authentic, always willing to share his preferences whether I asked for them or not. For example, he loved salsa music and knock-knock jokes and late-night playtime. Every night, right around midnight, he woke up to play games. My husband and I joked that the baby must have a wristwatch, because he was never late for our nightly date.

"I'm going to call him Midnight when he comes," I'd told Cory. "Midnight Tyler."

It amazed me just how perfectly this little being fit inside his own, untouched skin. He had such a strong presence. More than once, old ladies had stopped me the in street and pointed at my belly, saying, "That child is powerful. He has a strong destiny. He's going to be somebody!"

I believed it. He already was somebody—somebody confident and playful and engaging. I wondered if I'd been that way too before I was born—so clear about who I was. Maybe

I reveled in the ability to love and be loved unconditionally simply because I had the courage to exist.

Maybe we were all like that.

Maybe we were all born with complete clarity: the ability to do what is supposed to be impossible, to see beyond what is immediately visible, to know truths that seem unfathomable and to run into angels around every corner. Maybe the only reason we cycled down onto this planet was to have the opportunity to love one another recklessly and bask in the moment-by-moment glory of our own becoming.

Maybe this is the real nature of our being, even now.

But if that's true (and let's say for argument's sake, for the rest of this book, that it is), how do we learn to live from that space every day? What happens to that connectedness, that daring, that *flow* that we're gifted with on our way in here? For me, the connection had started to fade. I'd become cautious—thoughtful and habitual rather than mindful and free. The flow became turbulent and interrupted. Somewhere along the way, I started believing that I had to do something extra or be someone other than who I already was to be loved the way I wanted to be loved, even by my own self.

> Maybe we were all born with complete clarity: the ability to do what is supposed to be impossible, to see beyond what is immediately visible, to know truths that seem unfathomable and to run into angels around every corner.

I hadn't quite found the courage to be present with myself, as myself, without apology or excuse. At least not consistently. It requires a certain level of fearlessness to look at oneself in the mirror and really own the beauty of the miracle staring back. One's tolerance for beauty must first be raised in order to bear a sustained look. But only when that realization occurs is it possible to grow into the new life that's been calling. This is what I wanted to do, for myself and for my son. These were the changes that I'd thought about, prayed about, meditated on and fully intended to make. But nine months had slipped by and now he was almost here, even though absolutely I was no closer to being "there."

However, all of this is hindsight. In the early stages of labor, I couldn't have cared less about any of that stuff. At the time, all I wanted was to lie down and rest.

Exhausted, I sank onto the bed. Cory lay down with me, curled up at my back, cupping my belly in his hands. I inhaled a deep, relaxing breath. But rather than getting quieter, my thoughts got more jumbled. I felt like I sometimes do when I write and my hand can't keep up with the words scrolling through my mind. It was a familiar, if uncomfortable, feeling. For months, I'd even slept in these ongoing sentences, curled up on my side like a comma, with the baby, who was always the subject, protruding in front of me, and my husband, the predicate, hanging on for dear life from behind. Now here we were again, back in our familiar positions. Only nothing was the same. We were all transitioning. But into what?

By 6:00 a.m. we were both convinced that this wasn't another false alarm. The baby was coming. Cory called Angela, our doula, and after a few whispered words, passed the phone over to me.

"How do you feel?" she asked.

I said, "I feel like this hurts and if these contractions get any worse I'm gonna be really, really mad."

Angela sighed. I could almost see her smirking and rolling her eyes. "I'm on my way."

An hour later, Angela showed up and she, Cory, and I got down to the business of preparing our baby to be born. We walked up and down through the hills around our home. We danced to salsa music between contractions. We ate oatmeal, turkey bacon, and hashbrowns for energy. Cory held me up when my knees gave out under the pressure of a long, spiraling wave. He stood in tree pose, with his feet anchored to the earth, surrendering his body to hold us both up. Angela rubbed my back, murmuring to me to keep my face relaxed and coast on top of the waves.

Hours passed. The contractions sped up and got more intense. *Oh, God, the baby's coming!* I panicked. But then, as the afternoon wore on, the contractions all but disappeared. My labor stalled. Nearly an hour passed without a single contraction. *Oh God, the baby's not coming!* I panicked.

The mental contractions combined with the physical ones were almost too much. Finally, at one point when Cory was out of the room, Angela looked at me and said, "You're still in your head. Whatever is going on in there, you need to let it go. You need to lose your mind."

I looked at her like she'd gone first.

"To lose your mind means to surrender it," she said. "When you surrender, you can be fully in the experience of the body without being attached to it."

"I don't know if I can do that," I whined.

"You can," Angela assured me. "Let me ask you this— what is it that you haven't made peace with yet? What are you afraid of?"

Her question stopped me cold. I stopped panting, stopped feeling, stopped complaining. The thoughts that had been speeding through my mind began to slow down and soften in volume. Suddenly I could hear my breath. I could feel my heart. Angela was right: there was something heavy in there that I hadn't been aware of before.

"I'm afraid," I blurted out, "that I won't be able to take care of him like I should."

"Can you forgive yourself for believing in a thought like that?" she asked. "Can you let that thought go?"

When Angela asked the question, my stomach clenched. Letting go of that thought was just as scary as holding on to it. There was an emotional charge behind the thoughts of unworthiness, an investment of time, energy, and worry that didn't want to simply be dissolved.

How much of my life had I invested in false beliefs about myself? How long had I fought tooth and nail to hold on to an uncomfortable, but familiar, smallness? Had I avoided being present with my feelings because of what I feared I might find if I looked deep enough? But what would happen if I could stand still long enough to see myself truthfully, as the person I was in the moment, rather than who I thought I was based on who I believed I'd been in the past? This was the choice: release my old beliefs and allow the next stage of my life to emerge or stay where I was, mired in false ideas and fighting to have control over the uncontrollable.

Holding on to the old self can be seductive and comforting, like being with a lover who finishes your sentences for you and knows how every one of your stories ends. It provides a measure of assurance. It minimizes risk. But it also keeps you small.

Suddenly, I was terrified. I started to cry.

"Look," Angela said, "whatever you're holding on to, you have to let go. You need to be able to step back and allow this baby to come into this world the way that he needs to come. Your baby and your body are in perfect harmony. He knows exactly what he needs to get here. All you have to do is relax and surrender and let him come. Just let it be."

Relax. Surrender. Let it be.

Let myself be.

My son was clear in his purpose. He was prepared and ready, an active part of the process of life. He could ride the waves and direct them at the same time.

What about me?

Relax. Surrender. Let my self be.

This is the process of a woman being born. It is a process of becoming, of surrendering to what has always been there, waiting patiently for an opening to come through.

> To become a mother is to offer oneself over to possibility, to watch as the life around you and the life within you merge, take root, and blossom.

The birth of a child and the conscious birth of a mother are both gateways to the miraculous. To become a mother is to offer oneself over to possibility, to watch as the life around you and the life within you merge, take root, and blossom. Motherhood is the creative urge, the unlimited potential tucked away within the blossom's seed. It is also the soil into which that seed is dropped. The act of mothering, therefore, is a supreme act of self-recognition and faith, as well as love.

I needed to have the faith to look into myself, to recognize the goodness in whatever I found there, and receive it with love. I surrendered.

My stalled labor was not restarted with needles and medications, but with soft music, softer words, some tears, and a slowly opening heart. The contractions began again and suddenly jumped from eleven minutes apart to eight, and then down to six minutes and three minutes. Before we knew what had happened, the contractions were one to two minutes apart and we were flying down the 405 freeway toward UCLA Medical Center.

At the hospital, the midwife and the nurses tried to make me as comfortable as possible. But there wasn't really much that could help. We'd clearly stated in our birth plan that we were having a natural birth—no drugs or interventions. So we were on our own in a peaceful, dimly lit room, with a *waheguru* chant playing quietly in the background while my husband, our midwife, and our doula murmured encouraging words in my ears. It was hard for me to hear them, however, as I was too busy wailing at the top of my lungs, begging for intervention—divine, pharmaceutical, or otherwise.

But then it finally happened. During the transition phase, I left my mind. I entered into the trance state that I'd heard so much about, where it felt like God's hand was on me, squeezing the baby out of my body. God, apparently, has a vise grip.

The midwife and nurse sat in front of me while Cory sat behind me on the birthing bed and Angela stood at my side. I squatted, holding on to the birthing bar attached to the bed, bellowing out the pain after my body could no longer move.

After twenty-one hours of labor, at exactly midnight, Kingston James Tyler was born. True to form, he did not pause with his head showing, waiting politely for the next contraction to ease the rest of his body out into the world. He burst free all at once with a wail almost as loud as my own. During the first minute of the last day in August, he appeared into our lives as a beautiful bridge between past and future, between this world and the one behind it.

Kingston emerged from our birth red-faced, wide-eyed, and fully aware for the first time.

And, honestly, so did I.

The Gift of Presence

I swear, since seeing Your face,
the whole world is fraud and fantasy.
The garden is bewildered as to what is leaf
or blossom. The distracted birds
can't distinguish the birdseed from the
snare.

A house of love with no limits,
a presence more beautiful than Venus or the
moon,
a beauty whose image fills the mirror of the
heart.

— RUMI, *THE DIVANI SHAMSI TABRIZ XV*

A NEWBORN BABY IS A LIVING, BREATHING, SCREAMING, pooping meditation.

It takes some time, however, to come to that realization. At first, unless one already has a keenly developed sense of awareness, it feels like exactly the opposite. Sometime shortly after that last resolute push, mayhem ensues.

When Kingston popped out and the midwife placed him on my chest, I was astounded. My skin was the first skin that his had ever touched. The newness of him brought me near tears, feeling his cheek against my breast and the press of my husband's arms wrapped around us both as we leaned back into him, already cocooning.

It was as though nothing had existed before that moment and there was nothing waiting up ahead in the future. Everything made sense right now. *Of course this is why I'm here!* I thought. *How could it be otherwise?*

It felt like every gift inside me that I'd left dormant and dusty sprang to attention, enlivened by the possibility of the moment. I could do anything! And it wasn't just the flood of oxytocin in my blood talking. It was my truth: the truth of the moment and the truth of every moment—as long as I chose to stay awake and available to seeing it as such. With Kingston in my arms, I knew for certain that it could never have been any other way.

Pale and wrinkled, with a full head of wavy black hair but no lashes or brows, my son came into the world looking like a scrawny old man. He had swollen eyes, a trout pout, and feet so dark blue from lack of circulation they looked like they'd been rubbed with ink. As far as I could see, he was stunning. In fact, I'd never seen such flagrant beauty in all my life. Bewildered, distracted, I found myself standing in the doorway of a house of love with no limits. It was indescribable. There would be a trade-off for all this magnificence, a price to be paid, but I didn't know anything about that yet. I was still basking in the glow of that singular devotion that is unique to mothers and babies, oblivious to the rest of the world.

When Kingston snuggled up to my breast and began to nurse, time graciously seemed to stop altogether. My thoughts became like bugs trapped in a slab of amber, unearthed and held up to the sky: beautifully lit from within and perfectly still.

Those first moments were so rich. I felt like I was absorbing the joy through my breath and my skin and my eyes. It radiated out through my smile. The peace and well-being that enveloped us all seemed like it would last forever.

Then the nurses started coming into the room.

Each of them had a question, an answer, or an instruction. Kingston entertained them patiently, turning his head to gaze in the direction of each person who passed by. I, on the other hand, started getting impatient and uncomfortable. My attention got divided. My fossilized thoughts began to stir.

A nurse asked me if I wanted to take a shower, and that sounded like a good idea. I'd been covered in fluids that I didn't even know my body could make for nearly twenty-four hours. I desperately needed a good, long hot shower. So Cory took the baby and I headed into the bathroom with a nurse. I'd probably been under the water for two or three minutes when I felt weak and had to sit down on the bench against the shower wall. The next thing I knew, I was looking up at four or five nurses as they hovered over me with a wheelchair nearby and a bottle of smelling salts. At first I thought I was having one of those dreams where you're naked but everyone else around you is wearing clothes and going about their normal business. Then I realized that I'd actually passed out.

"You lost a lot of blood," one of the nurses told me. "Don't worry. It happens."

Of course, I started to worry. They wheeled me back through the bathroom door into the labor and delivery room. Now I was really bewildered and distracted, not to mention swollen and sore. My transcendent glow faded into a nice, ruddy, windswept flush—still there, but more manageable in the face of all real-world business that was suddenly pressing in on us.

Kingston somehow kept his equilibrium. I'd read that babies usually had about an hour or so of quiet alertness right after birth before fatigue set in and they drifted off to sleep. Not my son. He outlasted the midwife, Angela, both grandmas, the nurses, and even Cory. Everyone but me. Three and a half hours after he was born, my son finally drifted off into his first sleep. The new nurse on duty swaddled him and laid him on his side so I could see his face through the glass bassinet next to my bed. Only then did I settle down to sleep too.

Three or four hours later, the sun was up and it was time to really get down to business. There was a whirlwind of introductions, questions, instructions, tests, procedures, and visits. All I wanted was to snuggle up with my baby, close my eyes while I listened to his breath, and try to recapture some of the magic of those beautiful predawn hours. I didn't want to fill out any forms or talk to yet another staff member, as well intentioned as they were. I just wanted to go home and spend the next month or so staring into my baby's eyes. There didn't seem to be anything on the face of the earth that could possibly be more wonderful and delicious than lying down in my own bed in my own room at my own house with my own brand-new son. I would snuggle up under my sheets, facedown on my stomach (woo-hoo!), and sleep happily for the next...*two hours*.

Wait. Now even my daydreams were being altered. That thought startled me out of the thought I was already having. A feeling of unease bloomed inside my chest as my mind started to rev itself up again. The next thought that popped in was, once again, *What had I gotten myself into?*

Before Kingston was born, I used to ask other women, from a genuine sense of curiosity, what babies did all day. They're so tiny—immobile, really. They sleep fourteen out of the twenty-four hours available to them. On the face of it, the experience didn't seem like it could be that overwhelming. I'd worked way longer than ten hours a day at numerous points in my life. Surely I could to it again. For a writer, someone who lived in my imagination, lost in thought for hours at a time, I welcomed the "downtime" that I assumed I'd have during those fourteen hours. It's kind of embarrassing to admit it, but that's what I thought.

Somewhat belatedly, I realized that I was about to be buried in responsibility, one shovelful of new tasks at a time. And we hadn't even left the hospital yet. How would we manage? How would I be able to get it all done? Now my mind was really on a loop, the same incessant thoughts playing in heavy rotation.

Yet at the same time, there was Kingston, staring up at me, staring at his father, staring at all the other relatives trooping in and out as he patiently connected familiar voices to unfamiliar faces. In each interaction, he calmly gave the full measure of his focus to whatever was before him. And when he didn't like something that was happening to him, he promptly gave the full measure of his focus over to screaming at the top of his lungs. An infant's cry is somehow louder than a row of fire trucks careening down a New York City street at rush hour. At least to his mother. But then, the moment he was back in my arms and heard my voice shushing him, Kingston would hiccup and sigh and peacefully settle

> I was beginning to believe that he was anchored in grace.

back down. Whatever had been troubling him was quickly and completely dissolved from his experience.

What a wonderful trick, I thought. *He's got to teach me how to do that.*

In his quiet, in his crying, in all of his seeming newborn chaos, Kingston was anchored solidly in his experience of the moment. I was beginning to believe that he was anchored in grace. Perhaps this was one of the ways in which he'd brought a little piece of heaven with him when he came through.

I filed this thought away as we prepared to leave the hospital, a whole day early, and head home.

• • •

No one tells you that motherhood is simultaneously all the things that you ever dreamed it would be—and a thousand other things that you could never have had the imagination to dream up at all.

The baby is like the fairy godmother from Cinderella, waving a wand full of sneezy, sparkly dust over everything in sight and instantaneously transforming every area of your life down to its DNA. Nothing looks the same, has the same meaning or the same purpose. Everything is unfamiliar territory. New mothers usually look down at their babies and wonder, *My God, who are you?* No one tells you that, likely as not, you'll be looking in the mirror several times a day and asking the same question.

On the bright side, my experience of our birth and the joy of those first few weeks afterward made me aware of God again. I'd been on the outs with God for quite some time. After finding out that my father had HIV a couple of years earlier, I'd more or less cussed God out and written Him off as a fraud. I still went to church and everything, and I prayed when I really had to, but oh, man, was I pissed. With Kingston around, I started to soften. The face of God got kind of familiar again. I could see It all over the place—in the trees outside my door, in the sunset, and the sunrise, in the purr of my cat snuggled up on the bed at the baby's feet, and in the faces of the people walking up and down the street outside my door. I began to recognize God in all His clever disguises, as Mother Teresa so wisely put it.

But, at the same time, the minute-by-minute stress of parenting was also starting to take a toll. There wasn't a minute of the day that wasn't consumed by caring for the baby or thinking about what I was going to have to do next for the baby. Or if there was nothing to do at that exact moment, we used the reprieve to take pictures of the baby. The word *baby* became a noun, verb, or adjective in nearly every sentence that my husband and I uttered to each other. Except for the sentence "I'm exhausted." (This is Unspoken Transformation #1: Husband and Wife become Mama and Dada.)

To make matters worse, my body had turned into someone else's body, some old broad who had the nerve to look like somebody's mother. (This is Unspoken Transformation #2: Hot Young Thing takes a hiatus and leaves Perspiring, Frustrated Thirtysomething in her place.)

Everyone felt it was their duty to tell me all the things I obviously didn't know about raising my son, or else I'd be doing it different. (This is Unspoken Transformation #3: Perspiring, Frustrated Thirtysomething is apparently rendered incompetent by toxic birth hormones.)

Most of my friends quietly disappeared. The majority of them were actresses and models who hadn't quite gotten around to having children yet themselves. They all had big smiles and heartfelt congratulations, but not too much in common with me anymore. So they simply stopped calling and stopped coming by. (Unspoken Transformation #4: Crushing loneliness sets in.)

Kingston and I were all alone most days from early morning till sundown, going through changes, learning about each other as we learned all of the pauses and silences of the house too. We listened to the neighborhood cats wandering across the roof, creating a different kind of pitter-patter. I remember being grateful for the momentary company.

This is what life looked like in those first few weeks: No work. Few outings and even fewer friends. A baby who, in the ever-so-delicate terms of the attachment parenting gurus, could be called "high needs." Meaning that his enraged screams would have driven me to jump out of the dining room window if we lived in anything higher than a one-story bungalow. The peace and stillness of those first few hours felt like a dream when compared to the nonstop duties of the first few weeks.

Who ever tells you these things about motherhood?

> Who tells you that you'll experience bone-aching love, boredom, exhaustion, pain, fear, loneliness, frustration, joy, laughter, wonder, amazement, and doubt—not over the course of the baby's life, but sometime before lunch?

Who tells you that you'll experience bone-aching love, boredom, exhaustion, pain, fear, loneliness, frustration, joy, laughter, wonder, amazement, and doubt—not over the course of the baby's life, but sometime before lunch? It can be draining, to say the least. Under these circumstances, the mind can do some funny things. All the insights and revelations I'd thought I had seemed to dissolve in front of my eyes.

What, I began to wonder, am I doing with my life? How did I get here? Is this what it's going to be like? Constantly busy, constantly in motion, yet still wondering how I'm going to fill the hours ahead? How could the person I used to be disappear so far and so fast? And who's this new girl? I'm not too sure about her yet. There's so much at stake. But can I handle it all? Do I want to? What exactly do I want? I would've known the answer to that question before...

On and on I'd go, working myself into a frenzy of neurosis. Then Kingston would wake up or need to eat or seem like he could use a walk around the block and the chatter would stop. My focus would return and the moment would expand. But the minute my mind began to wander away from the task at hand, the thoughts came back, as loud and insistent as ever. But then one evening when Kingston was about six weeks old, we actually had a breakthrough.

We were having a real hard time. Kingston was colicky and he'd been screaming for nearly two hours. No one was home to help me and I had no idea what else I could possibly do for him. I'd tried nursing him, rocking him to sleep, walking with him, talking to him—everything I could think of, and nothing had worked. I put him down on the bed. Breathed. I picked him back up and started all over again. His cries seemed to get progressively louder and more pained. Pacing back and forth in our bedroom, I tried to figure out what more I could possibly do. How was I supposed to handle this?

"Please, Baby, tell me what you want," I pleaded. "I don't know how to help you."

His cries got louder.

Suddenly, I was furious—I was angry at the crying, at myself, at my aloneness, at my inability to soothe my own child, at the seemingly stagnant pool of water I was standing in that at one point had been my life. I couldn't take it anymore. I put the baby down roughly in his bassinet and started to walk out of the bedroom. Kingston must have sensed my frustration because he let out a desperate cry that sliced straight through my back as I walked away. No physical pain could hurt as deeply as hearing your child scream like that. But still I kept walking. I made it all the way out to the living room and threw myself down on the sofa. It was my intention to get away, to just sit there and let him cry for as long as I had to. But his cry had stuck me. I could feel it jutting out of my back, like a sword in a bad kung fu movie. About fifteen seconds after I sat down, I sprang up, hustled back into the bedroom, and gathered the baby gently in my arms. His crying eased and lost its frantic edge. He relaxed. But he didn't stop.

OK, I thought, *so this is it. This is what it's going to be. Can I be here?*

I pictured myself holding my son in the delivery room. It was a beautiful image, but it was only a memory. I couldn't get back to that moment ever again. However, I could stand in *this* moment and do everything in my power to love it just as much.

I relaxed too, and surrendered to the crying. I stopped trying to fix it or figure it out or do mental gymnastics to get my mind away from it. Instead, I breathed slowly as I cradled the baby close to my face, smelling the freshness of his skin and the salt in his brand-new baby tears. I stopped running from the sadness and stood still at the edge of my limit, letting my heart feel broken for the time being. Standing there fully engaged, I cried too, for both of us. But surprisingly, the tears didn't feel sad. They were tears of gratitude for even having the opportunity to be present, feeling the intensity of this love for another human being. They were tears of release.

"If you have anything to say," I whispered to Kingston, "I'm listening."

After a minute or two, a new awareness popped into my head.

Tired, it said. Need to sleep. Help me sleep.

Ha! That can't be it, my mind scoffed. I've tried to get this baby to sleep a dozen times. It can't be something as stupid and simple as that.

But that's what came, so I let go of the thoughts and went with the awareness.

"How?" I asked. Once again I got quiet and listened.

A few seconds later, something led me to sit down on the end of my bed and gently start bouncing up and down. In less than five minutes, Kingston was asleep.

I held him for a while, totally unable to believe how easy it had been to soothe him—when I knew how to be still, ask, and listen.

How many times had I thought that because my body was present with my son, I was doing enough? How many times had I missed the real truth and understanding in a situation, because my

It occurred to me that rather than mitigating the worries and fears, by putting undue attention on them I was actually making them grow.

mind was anywhere but in the moment? I'd routinely allowed my mind to get stuck in stories, fears, and doubts. Or else it was trapped in my "future," making elaborate plans and dodging all kinds of imaginary arrows. It occurred to me that rather than mitigating the worries and fears, by putting undue attention on them I was actually making them grow. It was like watering the weeds in my garden rather than the flowers.

The Buddhist monk Thich Nhat Hanh wrote,

> When a mother working in the kitchen hears the cries of her baby, she puts anything she is holding down and goes to the room of the baby, picks the baby up and holds the baby dearly in her arms. We do exactly the same thing when the seed of anger and fear manifest in us; our fear, our anger is our baby. Let us not try to suppress and to fight our fear and our anger. Let us recognize its presence; let us embrace it tenderly like a mother embracing her baby.
>
> When a mother embraces her baby, the energy of tenderness begins to penetrate into the body of the baby. The mother does not know, yet, what is the cause of the suffering of the baby, but the fact that she is holding the baby tenderly can already help. The energy of tenderness and compassion in a mother begins to penetrate into the body of the baby, and the baby gets some relief right away. The baby may stop crying. And if the mother knows how to continue the practice of holding the baby mindfully, tenderly, she will be able to discover the cause of the suffering of the baby.

To embrace fear and anger and misgivings right along with my child allowed me to embrace myself too. Placing tender, nonjudgmental attention on the situation and staying in the moment—holding it, rather than trying to hold on to it or, conversely, push it away—allowed something fresh and relevant to spring forth, what the old folks used to call mother's intuition. A little bit of compassion had some space to come through. And some insight came with it. This is what the old folks used to call grace. The rest could gently be let go.

That's what we did. We let the rest go and we both finally slept.

"If You Are Irritated by Every Rub, How Will You Ever Be Polished?": Choosing Harmony over Resentment

I've come to realize that the only people I ever have to forgive are the people who don't do things my way. And there seem to be a lot of them.

—EDWENE GAINES

"WOW! COME LOOK AT THIS."

Cory peered over my shoulder, trying to see what I was staring at on the laptop as I leaned against the kitchen counter near the sink.

"What is it?"

"This is unbelievable," I said, shaking my head. "How come I never knew this before?"

"What?"

"Listen to this: It's a little known fact that *postpartum depression* is actually the technical medical term for the condition known as 'lazy husband.'"

Somehow Cory didn't find this funny.

"How can you call me lazy when I haven't even done anything?" he asked.

Why, I wondered, do men tell on themselves this way?

My gaze slid down the counter like an icy beer bottle, plunking right against the dirty spoon that had been discarded next to the faucet. The spoon was not inside the sink. It wasn't in the dishwasher. It hadn't been cleaned, dried, and placed inside the silverware drawer where it actually belonged. No, the offending spoon was in its usual place, the place where it was most likely to cause me the greatest amount of annoyance because it was exactly where it *wasn't* supposed to be: on the counter.

Cory rolled his eyes at me. "Not that again."

"Yes, that again. I can't understand why you continue to do that when you know how much it irks me."

Truthfully, though, I believed I did know why my husband consistently left one grimy, cereal-encrusted spoon on my shining granite countertop. I believed that he did it for the same reason that men everywhere leave dirty underwear on the bedroom floor instead of in a hamper that is literally three feet away, or why they return from the supermarket loaded down with absolutely everything they can carry—except what you actually asked them to buy.

They simply don't like being told what to do.

In my theory there are many men who, though they deeply crave the love, reassurance, and convenience of domesticity, also fear losing that bit of themselves that they equate to freedom. They fear becoming neutered, having to walk through the world like a six-foot-tall Ken doll, good-looking on the outside but harboring a terrible secret within. So, in small ways that should be meaningless and imperceptible, they push back against the requests (demands?) of their spouses. In Cory's case, it was the *I'm-still-here-and-I'm-doing-it-my-way* spoon.

Suddenly, I was fuming. I wanted to shake him and yell, I'm still here too, right? I'm the one with a tiny person hanging on me all day. Why should doing something to make my life a little simpler be so difficult?

But before I could say any of that, Cory's phone began to chime and he, with a great show of relief, sprang to answer it.

"Hold that thought, babe," he whispered. "Hello? Hey, man!"

Kingston, who'd been draped across my arm, started doing his hungry kitten mewl. I sat down at the dining table to let the baby nurse, while listening to Cory go on and on to his friend Brian about the rigors of fatherhood.

"Yeah, man, it's tough," he said, popping a tortilla chip into his mouth. "But, you know, it gets better and better every day. The baby is doing great! He's just amazing. Seven weeks old now and he's already sleeping though the night."

"No, *you* sleep though the night," I butted in. "*We're* up."

Cory cupped his hand over the phone. "I'm sorry, babe, what did you say?"

At that point, it seemed like a good idea to get us out of the house for some fresh air.

These kinds of annoyances seem petty and silly to any rational mind. And they are. Until they're not.

The research says that the biggest stress on marriage (and, for women, the biggest correlating factor in the decision whether or not to file for divorce) is the perception of unfair division of household labor. That's right. It's not money or adultery or incompatibility that will ultimately do your relationship in—its dishes.

At first glance, that seemed ridiculous. It did to me, anyway. But the more I thought about it, the more sense it made.

Perhaps it speaks to a vague fear of becoming an indentured servant in one's own home, of not having one's concerns responded to in helpful and consistent ways. Perhaps it speaks to the overwhelm that so many people face when struggling to balance the demands of a growing family with other personal and professional obligations. Perhaps the offended party just feels plain old taken for granted.

Whatever the reason, these tiny tortures and resentments can wreck even the most stable of homes. And apparently, bringing children into the picture is like squirting kerosene onto the crackling bonfire. Statistics say that 30 percent of the couples who had babies in the US in 2009 (the year our son was born) would break up before the baby's second birthday. And that's not including the 10 percent of couples who called it quits before the pregnancy even ended.

Maybe I should've read some of those "Baby-Proof Your Marriage!" books that I'd smugly waddled past in the Childcare section of Barnes & Noble. But who knew that those first weeks of radical adjustment would be so awkward? The authors of the books, apparently. But not me.

Suddenly, my husband and I moved around each other like dance partners who never practiced. We both wanted to lead, but we were going in opposite directions. I'd never considered myself to be someone who made unreasonable demands on others. However, I'd recently come to the conclusion that when you have a seven-pound human attached to your body for twenty hours a day, any demand that you make is pretty reasonable.

Feeling grumpy and overburdened, I went into the bedroom to get Kingston changed again. I finally settled on an orange T-shirt with a peekaboo raccoon on the tummy and matching brown pants. He looked so adorable that I found myself smiling in spite of my grouchies. I took a few minutes to smooth down his hair with his little white baby brush, even though I knew it would immediately snap back into the long ringlets that always made strangers comment on what a pretty baby girl he was. Whatever. He was all ready to go.

I, on the other hand, looked a hot mess. But I quickly threw on a pair of jeans and a blue V-neck shirt that would allow me to pass for decent. That was as much energy as I could put into it at the moment.

I figured I'd talk my girlfriend Jasai into meeting us in Hollywood for tea. I dialed her number while simultaneously hunting for my shoes, purse, extra diapers, and car keys as the baby dangled kind of precariously from my right arm.

Praying that she wouldn't hear the unhappiness in my voice, I launched into my plan for our afternoon as soon as she picked up the phone. But before I could get to the part where I described the new teahouse on Larchmont that was absolutely calling our names, she stopped me.

"I'm sorry, sweetie. I can't do it today," she said.

"Aw, no," I groaned. "Why not?"

"I'm glad you asked. I wanted to find a way to tell you this and I wasn't quite sure how to do it. But as it turns out, Alex and I are breaking up."

"What happened?"

"It was me," she replied almost breezily. "All me. I met someone."

Well, now I really didn't know what to think. Jasai and Alex had been together more than ten years. They were raising two children together. And they seemed so compatible. Not too many people had the ability to keep up with Jasai's mind or her mouth. Bold, brilliant, and self-confident, Jasai was a samurai's blade. Alex had been the sheath that kept the blade comfortably and safely at rest. At least that's how it appeared. What could've happened? My mind darted back to the conversation I'd just been having with Cory. In relationships, you really can never tell where the truths lie.

"Is he packing or something?" I asked. "Is that why you can't come out?"

"No," she said. "He's still going to be living here for the time being. But I have a date this afternoon."

A date? Really? Why did I feel so blindsided by this?

"And how is Alex doing?"

"Well, at first he wasn't doing too good. But now he's coming around because he's started seeing someone else too."

Now I really didn't know what to say.

"Don't worry," Jasai said. "We'll get together later this week maybe and I'll tell you what actually happened. And then I can see the baby too."

"Oh. OK. That sounds good. I'll call you."

"OK, Pumpkin. I've got to go now. Bye!"

I sat there on the edge of the bed for a while, one shoe on, hair still undone, while the baby wriggled in my arms, trying to latch on to my breast right through my shirt.

Suddenly, I felt chained to my life; I was the caterpillar whose body has been melted down to goo inside the cocoon. Everybody loves the butterfly. Nobody pays attention to the fact that the caterpillar has to let herself be liquefied in order to become one. The only thing keeping her alive, keeping her insides in, is the very confines that she'll have to fight her way out of in order to be able to fly.

Pretty deep stuff. And all because of a spoon and a bad phone call?

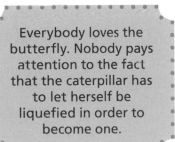

Everybody loves the butterfly. Nobody pays attention to the fact that the caterpillar has to let herself be liquefied in order to become one.

Couldn't be. I dialed again. I needed somebody to hear me out today.

My friend Dalila, a real honest-to-goodness butterfly, picked up on the first ring.

"Hey, darlin'," Dalila chirped. "I was just thinking about you."

"And here I am," I replied. "What are you and Phoenix doing today?"

"Cedi has Phoenix today. He doesn't bring her back until tomorrow evening. There's this red carpet thing I have to go to tonight but I'm just hanging out at home until then."

"Want to get together for some tea?"

"I'd love to! You'd have to come over here, though. But be warned—Kim is being a little attitudinal today."

Kim, Dalila's live-in girlfriend, seemed to be attitudinal on a pretty regular basis.

"What happened this time?" I asked.

Dalila sighed. "Who knows? Well, actually I do know. She's experiencing some of my behaviors as emotional triggers right now."

"Huh?"

"She thinks I take her for granted because she does the majority of the housework and I let her."

"Why do you let her?" I asked. I was really curious about that.

"Because clutter isn't one of my triggers."

"I see."

"It's not for me, it is for Kim. She needs things to be ordered in a certain way to feel comfortable. And I understand that. But I have so many other things to focus on in a given day that dusting and mopping aren't a high priority for me."

"I see."

Dalila lowered her voice. "Kim got very upset the other day. When I came home, she was just sitting here in the dark waiting for me. She'd made a pie chart showing exactly how much more housework she does than me. She wanted me to see specifically which areas I'm lagging behind in."

"A pie chart?"

"Yes, girl, a pie chart."

"You've got to be kidding me!" I laughed so loud I startled the baby and he started fussing.

"No, ma'am, I am not kidding. Kim also made another chart on an Excel spreadsheet outlining a new work schedule. She hung it up on the refrigerator and now every time one of us completes a chore, we have to initial next to the column where the chore is denoted."

"Wow. That's deep." I wondered how Cory might like living with Kim. "Does that kind of thing work for you?"

"Personally, I'd rather just hire a maid. But neither of us has any money right now."

"You know what I mean."

Dalila sighed. "I understand, though. I recognize that it's a pendulum swing. In her other relationships, Kim never knew how to set boundaries. Now she does. It's all working itself out, I guess. Our therapist thinks that it is too. Do you still want to come over?"

"Um, how about later in the week?"

I heard Dalila snorting as she tried to hold in her laughter.

"Yeah, that does sound like a better idea."

Well, I thought as I hung up the phone, *that relationship isn't long for this world either.*

What was going on? It was like being visited by the Ghost of Christmas Past and the Ghost of Christmas Future in the same afternoon. I felt like God was trying to warn me or punish me, but I couldn't tell which one. There was obviously a message that I was supposed to be getting that had swept right over my head. Maybe God was telling me to make Cory a pie chart. Probably not, though.

I took so long making up my mind on what to do that Kingston started drifting off to sleep in my arms. I figured I'd use the quiet time to make one more call. I called my friend Crystal.

"Hey, lady, what's up?"

I smiled to hear the song in Crystal's voice. It made me want to cry too.

"I'm having a little bit of a hard day," I mumbled. "I just needed to hear a cheerful voice."

"Oh." Crystal was instantly attentive. "What happened?"

Now that I finally had someone to listen to me, I didn't know what to say. *My husband won't put away his socks or his silverware? He doesn't hear the baby or me when we cry?* Could that even be considered a fair critique if I know I'm crying too softly to be heard? But how could I say such self-indulgent things to Crystal, whose fiancé, the father of her two-year-old daughter and stepfather to her fifteen-year-old son, had recently broken off the engagement and left home because he needed "space." I had a good husband. Was I really going to sit there and complain about my petty anxieties and resentments?

"I guess I'm just feeling invisible today," I whispered.

And that was the truth.

"Why?" she asked.

Another great question. How could I say what I was feeling? That I, Kuwana Haulsey, was the woman who had braved riots while living in Kenya and followed in the footsteps of South African freedom fighters, even though their trail led straight through a mountain cemetery to their graves. I was the woman who'd sailed a mile out into the Indian Ocean and then gotten out to walk along the shallow sea shelf; I'd literally walked atop the ocean. I was the woman who wrote books and acted in plays and had climbed Kilimanjaro. I'd been the beautiful American woman, sitting alone in a smoky Parisian café, writing again, while stunning Italian men tried to lure my attention away from the scribbles on my napkin and the pen in my hand. I was the woman who'd sat silently underground in the slave caves of Zanzibar, feeling the ancestors waiting at my back, while trying to find the words to write down what I thought I heard them saying.

Now I couldn't even find my other shoe.

Now I was the woman who sat on the end of her bed, confused, hair still undone, trying to figure out why it felt so difficult to just get out of the house. I was the woman who was worried about God-damned spoons.

> I was the woman who'd sailed a mile out into the Indian Ocean and then gotten out to walk along the shallow sea shelf; I'd literally walked atop the ocean.

Could it be, I heard my little inner voice say just then, that Cory and his spoon have very little to do with your existential quandary? Maybe God is speaking to you, but not about him.

Very quietly, I said to Crystal, "I think I just want to be seen. I've been very angry and kind of a brat today because I've been feeling like nobody cares about what I need anymore. It's my job to be there for Kingston and make sure he has everything that he needs. But it would be nice to have someone to do that for me too. That's all. Is that crazy?"

"Of course not," Crystal said. "Trust me, I don't know anyone who hasn't felt that way. In fact, I'm going to send you a story I wrote. I think I'm going to make it into a blog or something. It's pretty funny. I think it will cheer you up."

As soon as we ended our conversation, she e-mailed me a link to her story. But before I could log on to my computer, Kingston woke up from his catnap and started to grumble. I was about to close the laptop to tend to the baby when Cory walked into the bedroom.

"What are you guys doing in here?" he asked.

"I was going to do some reading, but..."

"You go ahead. Take your time." Cory smiled at me, picked the baby up, and walked back out of the room.

Feeling grateful, and a little guilty for being so mean, I opened my computer to find a new message in my inbox. I clicked on the link and immediately got the smile that Crystal promised:

Some days, I'd like to revert back to my toddlerhood. Like now, I wish I could ignore a few people; just pretend I don't hear them or see them. It may sound silly because, as an adult, certainly I know better. I know how to communicate. But in those moments when I don't feel heard or understood, I admit that I've found myself wishing I could throw a toddler tantrum. NOTE: I'm not talking about an adult tantrum. As a grown woman you'll be labeled manic-depressive, bipolar, or plain crazy for acting out. You'll be told, "Oh, you must be on your period," as if that statement has anything to do with wanting to be heard or understood.

Lately, I've been studying my daughter during and after her temper tantrums. How free and relieved she looks after each one. The other day I found myself saying, "Must be nice!" as I watched her scream at the top of her lungs because she was denied a piece of gum. I remember wondering what she would do if I started screaming with her.

It made me think: What would it be like to just let go and throw a good old-fashioned tantrum? It might happen something like this:

Scenario 1: My boss/supervisor reaches to hand me work that I don't feel like doing at the moment. I have nothing against her, but I'm not in the mood to do it right now. Maybe later. She tries placing the pile of papers in my hand.

Toddler Tantrum #1: I move my hand and let the pile drop to the floor, then run away laughing. When she tries to hand it to me again I say, "I don't want that!" The more she tries handing the papers to me the louder I yell, "I don't want that!" The boss then tries putting the pile of work on my desk. This frustrates me because I've already made it known that I don't want to do it, so I knock the papers on the floor.

My boss seems angry at this point and begins to reprimand me. She even mentions my job being in jeopardy. I can't take it anymore! Clearly my boss doesn't understand my wishes. So, I throw myself down on the floor and begin to kick and fling my arms around, screaming at the top of my lungs, "I DON'T WANNA DO IT RIGHT NOW. JUST GIVE ME A SECOND! NOT NOW, NOT NOW!" This, of course, scares the shit out of my boss, who has no choice but to walk away and let me be. Which is what I asked for from the very beginning. I lie there on the floor for a few more seconds and happen to notice the pile lying on the floor next to me. I take a look at the work and decide…I can do it now. I walk to my boss's desk, hand her the finished work, and say, "Sorry." *End of story.*

Scenario 2: My beloved and I are supposed to be having "alone time." I ask him if he could please refill my glass of wine. He sweetly says yes, but something on television has his attention. I wait patiently for a few minutes and then ask him again. "Hold on, babe," is what he tells me. Again I patiently wait. I move closer to him in hopes of snagging his attention. I tap him on the leg and he says (without even looking at me), "Give me a sec, babe." At this point it's more about him ignoring me than It is the glass of wine. I stand in front of the television in hopes of being seen and heard. He is now annoyed and bobs his head from side to side trying to catch a glimpse of the screen.

Toddler Tantrum #2: I take my glass and throw it. *End of story.*

Scenario 3: Another adult is chastising me. This adult is explaining why what I did was wrong or wasn't the best decision I could've made. Each time I try telling him my side of the story, he keeps going back to his own side. Finally, I feel as if it's better to just be quiet than to continue on with the conversation. But being quiet doesn't settle my soul.

Toddler Tantrum #3: A) I stare at this person and pretend to not understand a word he's saying. I blink a few times, but say absolutely nothing; B) I play possum. I start slinking down in my seat as if I'm either falling asleep or dying; C) I start crying uncontrollably. I let snot run down my nose and make sure to open my mouth wide without any sound for a few seconds. When the sound finally does come out, I let it ricochet off the walls to make sure that everyone else can hear exactly what this mean, horrible man is doing to me. Just let it all hang out! *End of story.*

Now, I'm not condoning any of these behaviors. When my kids do them they're reprimanded or put in time-out. But if I can be completely honest: I understand! There are

moments I, too, want to act out, especially if it will mean
that I'm finally being heard, understood, and paid appropriate attention. There are many days I'd like to have a
temper tantrum—without being worried about someone
calling me a name for having one.

Being understood is a precious thing. It can ease the suffer-
ing of isolation to a simple ache or sweep aside a heavy web
of shame and false expectations that looks like "not good
enough." Being understood is a lifesaving necessity. But I
was coming to realize that the one thing that held far greater
importance was to honestly be able to say that you understood yourself.

To understand yourself is to stop dumping your trash on
someone else's lawn and then calling them a slob behind their
back for not maintaining their property. It means releasing
"he should," "he needs to," and "why won't he" and replac-
ing them with "I will."

I wanted to understand
myself and my truth in an
honest, unselfconscious way.
Sort of. But some things

> Being understood is
> a lifesaving necessity.

hurt too much. There were way too many variables hovering
just out of reach of my conscious thought. I also knew that
expecting someone else to change so that I could be content
was madness.

The only answer that could possibly be meaningful for me

or anybody else required me to make a stand inside my own spirit and ask myself the most fundamental of questions: who are you now and what do you want?

Very interesting questions with no clear answers. At least not yet.

A Life of Everyday Miracles: Embracing a Transcendent Vision

There is no passion to be found in settling for a life that is less than the one you are capable of living.

—NELSON MANDELA

WE LIVE IN A TIME AND A CULTURE WHERE WHO YOU ARE is synonymous with what you do. We rarely separate the two. It's like the red and white stripes on a barber's pole; one defines the other. If you take one away, there appears to be nothing left of what you were originally looking at. The singularity creates something altogether different. Or so it seems. We live, eat, breathe, and get our sense of self-worth from our ability to say, I am this or I am that. We say with pride, "People see me as a leader" or "I am a nurse" or "I'm a teacher" or "I'm the executive, the decision maker."

This sense of identification and purpose can be a beautiful thing. On the other hand, how we experience this consciousness may depend largely on which end of the food chain we happen to occupy. Does your station in life afford you a weighty, nuanced definition? Or are you like the proverbial tree in the forest that no one notices when it comes crashing down? You work and work and work all day, but because no one sees you and no one acknowledges or celebrates your contribution, it feels like maybe you haven't made one.

For most of my life, I considered myself an artist. Wholly an artist. Everything I did revolved around exploring, creating, expressing, becoming something new. In that identity, I felt recognized and appreciated and free. Every moment of self-expression was something of a miracle, a new opportunity to create. My self-worth arose from my

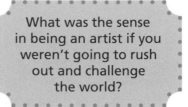

What was the sense in being an artist if you weren't going to rush out and challenge the world?

vision of the world as malleable, completely open to my interpretation. Because, as an artist, what were you if not a sculptor of reality, someone daring and powerful? What was the sense in being an artist if you weren't going to rush out and challenge the world?

Did Emily Brontë agonize over the laundry, and cut short her writing time because "if she didn't do it, it wasn't going to get done"? Probably not. Did Franz Kafka spend his precious days crawling along in a carpool lane just to get home, collapse on the couch, and lie there exhausted until morning? No. They were soldiers who flung themselves, headlong, into the bloody war of art. And, ultimately, they won. They may have died prematurely, but they died victorious. In my mind, that's what counted.

Who would I be if I wasn't living on the edge of certainty, painting pictures of life in large swirls and bright colors? Without that strange life, would I cease to exist on some level, fading away into normalcy until there was hardly anything left? These were not conscious thoughts, but rather feelings that lodged themselves inside my chest whenever I found myself alone in the dark, early hours of the morning.

On one of those mornings, with Kingston curled up in my arms, I paced through our house and backyard, then back and forth outside, up through the hills. The sky was a stunning mix of amber and rose, the kind of light that settles onto your body, to be carried like a shawl over your shoulders. It was the kind of light that sometimes slips over the city when the Santa Ana winds are blowing hot and you know there are brush fires burning somewhere close by. It's beautiful and unsettling at the same time.

That was a good description of how I felt as we walked quietly through our neighborhood. As beautiful as the moment was, it was also foreign. The quiet and the predictability were so opposite of my vision of myself. In fact, to be so domestic and content actually felt a little dangerous, a little subversive. Who was this lady with the uncombed hair and the lumpy gray sweater? Whoever she was, she didn't catch people off guard or leave them wondering—maybe even a little suspicious—about what she'd do next.

No. She was *nice*. She had new priorities.

Now everything was different and a little more complex. Life required planning. Even doing something simple like taking the baby out for a walk usually became a big deal, a Broadway production of socks and diapers and lotions and hats and sweaters and lighter sweaters just in case the temperature changed and bags and carriers. It was more than I had bargained for and such a huge departure for me, the person who would pick up and travel the world on a whim.

The girl I used to be was in love with mystery. She believed in huge, life-changing miracles. Being an artist had been my doorway to the miraculous. As Kingston and I walked, I thought back to a time that seemed, from my new vantage point, like ancient history. But it wasn't. It was my life. There was an artist at my core, and, no matter how unconsciously, I'd always believed that she defined me.

Truthfully, I wasn't exactly sure who I was without my self-imposed definitions. In my mind the interesting part of my story, the part that mattered, began when I was twenty years old and I decided to write my first book.

● ● ●

I'd been living in Brooklyn in a tiny, one-bedroom walk-up on Bond Street between Atlantic Avenue and Pacific Avenue. That was the headquarters for my takeover of Broadway. Back then I lived for the theater—the smell, the lights, the proscenium, and everything that went into creating the theater space. I was working hard toward being part of a community of actors who I felt were telling the stories of our times. From the space of that tiny apartment I plotted and planned how I was going to leap off into that world. Unfortunately, my headquarters was very messy. One afternoon, when I just couldn't take it anymore, I decided to clean.

In the bedroom, I sorted through piles of papers that had been taking up space in my closet. I wanted to prune everything that was getting in my way. As I leafed through the stacks, my mind drifted back to the last audition that I had. Did I do well? Did they like me? Would they call me in for another meeting? Did I need a new agent? I should be going out on more calls and I wasn't. Was something wrong?

I absently fingered the pieces of paper I was sorting, tossing most of them in the trash bin, not really giving it too much thought. But something turned my attention back to the task and caused me to look down at the paper in my hand. It was a college admissions letter that I'd gotten three years prior and had saved, though I couldn't tell you why. The letter said, "Congratulations! You have been accepted into the United States International University." Well, I'd never even applied to the United States International University, so I never thought seriously about going there. Because of my GPA, I'd been preemptively accepted to a number of schools that I couldn't have cared less about. My aspirations were set a little higher—NYU, to be exact. I'd been invited to attend the famed Tisch School of the Arts and had every intention of going. (Except that I'd never actually shown up there that fall, which was another long story by itself).

I'd probably saved that piece of paper from USIU because something about the school appealed to me. Maybe it was the fact that the university had campuses in Mexico, London, and Kenya. Back then, I'd never been out of the country but had always wanted to travel. In lieu of actually going anywhere, I guess I'd just folded up the paper and tucked it away.

Over the course of the three intervening years I'd forgotten that the letter even existed. And yet, there it was, popping back up on a sunny afternoon as I sat on my bedroom floor in front of my canopy bed, going through pieces of my past. I looked at the letter and smiled to myself, thinking, *Hmmm, it would be nice to move to Africa to the campus in Nairobi. I could go to school there. That would be pretty awesome. And I could even write a book about it.*

As that thought filtered into my brain, I stopped breathing. Everything around me faded from view as a download of information flooded my mind. It came too quickly for me to process, or to even say I "thought" something. But, nevertheless, a story unfolded right there in that moment. It was a story of a girl who was young and afraid and alone in the world. That girl had very specific goals in mind for herself. She insisted on being more than the people in her life believed that she could be. As I sat there, the entire plot for a book filtered through my awareness in the space of a few seconds. A world opened up to me that I hadn't even known existed. I saw the girl whom I would be writing about. I felt her heart. I saw the things that had been done to her, the place where she lived, and the people she lived with.

I saw her tribesmen, and knew that they were good people, people of honor and powerful belief systems. I saw them walking the African plains, striding proudly through the scrub, with acacia trees jutting up in the distance. I saw the girl's face. She was struggling to win a miracle in the same way that I was. And I saw her succeeding the way I wanted to succeed.

Slowly, the sunlight began to filter back into the room. But everything looked different now, heightened: the particles of dust floating through the air from the upended boxes, the glow of the late-afternoon light through the window, the cats snuggled into the rumpled sheets. They swatted softly at each other while they waited for me to be done with whatever was distracting me from our playtime. Nothing in the room had changed, except me.

I'd quite literally witnessed a new vision for my reality. My twenty-year-old mind didn't question it. I just assumed that if the vision came to me, it was for me. And if it was for me, nothing could keep me from it. I made the decision right then and there to leave my home and my family to move to Africa.

Within two months, I had quit my job, packed up my apartment, and activated a new student file with the United States International University. I told them I was coming to start for the summer quarter.

> I was being given the opportunity to have a voice, to say something that seemed important.

No one really believed that I'd go until I left. No one in my world went further from the Bronx than Queens or Brooklyn. It was unthinkable to travel to the other side of the world on a hunch. But I was going. I packed with a heavy heart, covering everything in my teeny apartment with tears. But it never occurred to me not to go. I was being given the opportunity to have a voice, to say something that seemed important. That's what I believed, what I was willing to stake everything on. Two months later, I stepped aboard an American Airlines flight and took off for Nairobi.

I remember the plane gliding in for a landing and seeing the soft-looking soil, brick red in some parts and smoothed and black like coffee in other parts. Palm fronds and vibrant green grasses that looked as tall as a man dotted the lush farmland outside the airport. It was all so good and delicious and full of promise.

I stepped off the plane into a warm, lovely dry heat. It wasn't nearly as hot as I thought it was going to be. It was hotter in Florida, where I'd lived before, so I was pleasantly surprised. After some finagling I managed to grab a taxi—a battered, rusty pickup truck with a Jamaican flag painted on the door. We headed off down the highway, driving by the city center and around through the hills, passing concrete houses with the corrugated tin roofs on top. Women walked with plastic basins and jugs on their heads. Little boys and girls ran around in their blue-and-white school uniforms. Some uniforms were in tatters, while others were crisp and clean. Either way, the children appeared to be happy and full of laughter.

After about a half hour of driving, we turned off the main road past Safari Park Luxury Hotel. At first I thought, *Hey, this isn't bad*. I assumed that I'd be making my artistic mark from the lap of luxury, like the people strolling behind the gates of the palatial hotel compound. But then the taxi kept going around a twisty bend. As soon as we got around the curve in the road where the Safari Park property ended, the asphalt ended too.

The rest of the road (if one could still call it that) was a dusty, rooster-comb-red slash of dirt. We bounced along, with dust kicking back into my face, smothering me through the open windows like a thick, red blanket. I braced myself against the roof of the pickup truck with my hand, trying not to fly up and hit the top of my head. I wanted to ask the driver to slow down a little, but I was afraid. I didn't dare. He wasn't even going that fast. The road was just that bad. After about a half mile we finally reached the gates of the United States International University.

A guard swung the gates wide open, and I got my first look at our campus, with the flame trees and beautiful palms, and fields going back as far as I could see behind buildings. Boys killed cobras in those fields, but I didn't know that yet. I would find that out in the days to come as I walked through those fields trying to get to my classes.

After finally locating the campus administrators, I was sent back the way I had come to an area called Parklands, where the dorms were. This entailed another dusty bus trip, where people politely tried to make room for my huge, ugly trunk full of things that I immediately realized I would never need. When we arrived in Parklands, the RA informed me, after having traveled for twenty-four hours straight all the way to the other side of the world where I knew no one and no one knew me, that the dorms were full. There was no room in the inn. I was out of luck.

> When you're on a mission in your own mind, a mission that's bigger than you are, that's full of wonder and importance, you belong.

The young man felt badly for me and asked me to sit outside his office while he tried to figure out an alternative. So there I was, all alone in Nairobi, with nowhere to stay. All I had was that battered old steamer trunk, covered in what looked like a quarter inch of red soot. I sat outside the RA's office on a rickety wooden chair feeling miserable. Inside, the phone rang. The murmur of his voice seeped through the door as I closed my eyes and breathed deep. Little pinpricks of panic tried to bleed through with his conversation, but I breathed them away. *I am here for a reason,* I reminded myself. *I am here for a purpose. There is nothing in this situation that cannot work out for me. There is some place here for me. I do belong here.*

What a huge declaration for me. I do belong. That's not something that I'd always been able to say, before or since. I belong. When you're on a mission in your own mind, a mission that's bigger than you are, that's full of wonder and importance, you belong. You don't necessarily belong to people, places, organizations, or schools. You belong to life. You belong in the heart of God. As I sat in that hot hallway, I realized that this expectant, somewhat uncomfortable feeling was simply how it felt to live and walk and move and dance in the heart of God. And truly, what could harm me there?

After a few moments, the RA called me back inside.

As he put the phone back down in its cradle he said, "Well, Ms. Haulsey, you're not going to believe this, but a bed has opened up. It's the last bed that we have on campus, and if you want it it's yours. Would you like it?"

"Yes," I said, as if the news were the most natural thing in the world. "Of course. I'll take it."

The RA had just begun to type up my paperwork on his typewriter when another girl walked in behind me and said, "Mr. Jonathan, they told me in the main office to come see you because I need a room in the flats. Do you have anything at all available?"

"No," said Mr. Jonathan, the RA. "We have nothing. You have to try back again next semester."

The girl hung her head and left. I felt bad for her. But I also fully believed that my room had been waiting for me to show up and claim it. And I did. Life gives you what you expect and what you're willing to accept, nothing more and nothing less.

The flat in Parklands was in a five-story walk-up building and I was on the fourth floor. Four rangy boys stumbled up the stairs behind me, toting my ridiculous trunk. When we got to the fourth floor, I opened the door and saw that both of my flatmates, Lorraine and Juliet, were waiting.

"Habari yako," called Lorraine.

She was one of the cutest girls I had ever seen, so petite and welcoming. I soon learned that Lorraine was everybody's favorite. She was sweet, demure, and well spoken. The ideal woman in these parts. (It was funny that we should be put together. I was *so not* any of those things.) Juliet was quiet. She had a round, motherly face and would later take to doing things like making my bed when I was too lazy to do it myself. They both opened their arms to me and immediately made me family.

I spent my first couple of days in Nairobi wandering the marketplace across from our flats, dodging through the narrow passageways, which had stalls on either side. Sometimes the stalls were just blankets piled high with grains and vegetables and roots. Haggling people squeezed into every available space. The smell of wood and trash burning, fish cooking, and overripe fruit commingled with the insistent voices and the crush of sweating bodies. As I walked, I saw women haggling over cloth and beans and collards. A woman up ahead had just finished grousing with a fruit seller. Her determination had won her a nice, fat bunch of baby bananas at a very good price, judging by the smug smile on her face. She put the bananas in the basket on the top of her head and strutted off. I walked behind, watching her balance this huge basket of food so effortlessly on her crown, with her prize bananas perched at the top. Unbeknown to the woman, a naughty monkey was following her too. I saw him but she didn't.

The monkey jumped from beam to beam to beam along the rafters in the roof. He scampered down a wooden pole when she wasn't looking and snatched those bananas right off the top of her head. She never even noticed. Then the monkey ran back up the pole and sat in the rafters, cackling and screeching his delight. The laughter caught the woman's attention and, upon realizing that the cheeky monkey had outsmarted her, she began to tell the monkey off. Offended, the monkey threw one of the woman's own bananas back at her, which really started a row.

I laughed too, even though laughing made me cough because the air was so thick with the mash-up of smells and incense smoke and sunlight. I laughed from the sheer delight of knowing that this was where I belonged. This was what I was supposed to be doing. Every sight, every sound, was a new word on a page in my mind.

It was very clear to me that I needed to get to work. Therefore, after taking a brief holiday with all my new friends to the Mombasa coast because, well, it was college, after all, I began the task of researching for my book. My initial research consisted of introducing myself to people on the long bus ride to campus and asking for help. (Luckily for me, it was an American university where English was the common language. So I didn't have to fumble around trying to get people to understand my nonexistent Swahili.) My pitch went something like this:

"Hi. My name is Kuwana. I'm from New York. What's

your name? Okay, that's good. I have a question for you, and I really hope you can help me. I'm writing a book. And the people in the book don't live in the city. They live in the country, off the land. They're traditionalists. They also circumcise their daughters at a very young age and they marry them off pretty young, too. I know these people, but I don't know who they are. Oh, one more thing—they live very close with their animals in small villages. They herd cattle and I see goats and sheep and maybe some dogs. I'm not too sure about the dogs, but that's what I think. That's all I know. Do think you could help me?"

I asked this question of Lorraine first.

"Oh, that's easy," she answered. "That's the Samburu. They live in the highlands. It's pretty far away and I don't know if you can get there, but that's who you're talking about."

It was almost surprising for the answer to come that easily. But then again it wasn't. I *believed* I was supposed to get my answers. The ease with which the answers came didn't feel miraculous or unusual in any way. It felt right. I believed wholeheartedly in alignment, and that's what showed up.

As I continued to meet people on campus I'd ask the same question. Invariably, I got the same response: "Oh, that's the Samburu tribe."

The next step was to somehow make it to the highlands at the edge of the Rift Valley. I wasn't quite sure how to get the access that I needed. As I was finding out, the Samburu were notoriously mysterious and insular. Again I asked for help.

"Lorraine, I need to get up to the highlands and I don't know how to get there. I don't even know where that is," I said to her one day as we walked along the path through the tall grasses toward our classroom. "What do you suggest I do?"

Lorraine walked beside me with her skirt rustling in the breeze and her perfectly curled hair brushing her shoulders.

She said, "Oh, my, my, my... That's a tricky one. I'm not sure if this will help, *bwana*, but there's a travel agent that I know. You could ask him how you could get the highlands."

"Okay! That would be great."

Lorraine wrote down a name and handed me the little slip of paper. Right after class, I raced to the city center. There were no school buses going back to town at that time, so I had to risk the threat of bandits and walk the road to the nearest matatu station. Most matatus were nine-passenger minivans that had been repurposed to carry fifteen or sixteen people at a time. They were so crowded that strangers would sometimes even sit in your lap. I boarded the matatu and placed my book bag over my thighs, just in case. People were squeezed into crevices and corners, hunched over in the doorway spaces, and even hanging out the open doors.

The matatu conductor hung out the side door, his clothes whipping in the wind, making him look like a thin, brown flagpole. It was so crowded I could barely breathe. At the same time, I felt incredible, like there was fire coursing through my body. I was on the right track. It was like being a detective, searching out clues. If I could find my way to town and back by myself, I'd be in business.

The matatu pulled into the city center and I squeezed my way out, elbowing past a wall of people. It was worse than any New York subway train I'd ever been on. I jumped down, pulling my little leather book bag out behind me. Following a hunch, more than any written directions, I set out for a street that I'd never heard of, in a place I'd never been before, to meet some people I didn't know, who weren't expecting me, because they were going to be my link to the next step in the unfolding of this grand vision.

Finally, after a number of wrong turns I arrived at the travel agent's office. A little bell jingled over my head as I walked in and the man in front of me looked up from his place at his desk. He took one look at my clothes, smiled, and called out, "Jambo!"

Jambo was how people greeted foreigners and tourists, as opposed to *habari yako*, which was how they greeted each other. I could almost see the man thinking *muzungu,* which technically meant "white man," but could be applied to any-one in hiking boots and khaki shorts, with a map in their hand. I wasn't offended.

"Hello," I called back, walking over. "My name is Kuwana. My friend Lorraine sent me here to see Paul. Is he around?"

Just then, a happy-looking middle-aged gentleman stepped

in through the back door and said, "That is me. May I help you, miss?"

Ah, so this was my co-conspirator. I smiled even wider. "My friend Lorraine sent me to come look for you. I want to travel to the highlands to live with the Samburu for a while and she said that you might be able to help me."

"Oh, but of course! I can arrange a wonderful tour of the Rift Valley for you. It is spectacular at this time of year—"

"Oh, no, no, no, no," I interrupted. "I can't do a tour. I want nothing of the kind. I'm writing a book, a very serious novel. This is a literary venture, you understand. It has to be real and gritty."

"I see," he said, nodding gravely.

"I'm looking for authenticity. So I need to live out in the bush with the people and become one of them. How do I do that?"

How he didn't toss me out of his office on my ass, I will never know. Instead, Paul pushed back in his chair and studied me for a moment. Then he put his hands behind his head and said, "Huh! Be one of the people? Eh, *bwana*, that's harder than it sounds. They don't trust too many outsiders, girls like you. I don't know. Let me think about that a little while longer."

Fair enough. I had about fifteen more minutes. I sat down quietly in one of the little metal chairs by the front door to let him think.

Finally, he called me back over and said, "Well, as luck

would have it for you, I'm from those sides. My sister still lives there and I was planning a trip home next week. If you want, you can come with me."

But of course.

"I would love to come with you," I said. "That would be wonderful! When do we leave?"

Some might call this a bit crazy, a bit too trusting and naïve. Some might say that I asked for a little bit of trouble, even. I didn't see any of that. I only saw myself as fulfilling my part in a great adventure, and anyone who was going to become part of that vision was also helping themselves to fulfill their own good. That was my truth.

I traveled with Paul to the highlands that next week, and again two or three times during the course of my stay in Nairobi. I lived with Samburu people, determined to learn what it meant to be Samburu, nomads and traditionalists in the modern world. It astounded me to be experiencing, in person, the same things that I'd seen in my mind, while sitting in my little Brooklyn apartment more than 8,000 miles away. I found that, truly, God had not lied to me. Everything was as it had been shown to me. This confirmation started me on the path to being a writer, which I'd never, ever considered before. That, in and of itself, was something of a minor miracle.

Over the course of the year, I came face-to-face with many such miracles, though they didn't seem miraculous at the time. They seemed like normal, natural happenings, as expected as waking up in the morning and having a cup of tea or brushing my teeth.

As I learned more about all the different people, their languages and traditions and all the things that I could never really lay claim to, I became aware of the depth of the reward that comes when you agree to take a risk and believe in the miracle. I vowed to myself that I would always live from that space of trust, where doubt has no room to define you, and purpose is all that matters. Intuitively, I understood that living my purpose would not only dictate the quality of my life, but could also directly affect the people all over the world with whom I was connected. I could say things, dare things, which could then open doors for others. I was absolutely sure of that fact, and ready to risk everything to make that truth my reality.

All told, I spent almost a year living in Kenya. As the months flew by and I continued to conduct my research, my new way of life became ingrained within me, not just something I slipped on and off for the sake of some artsy-fartsy project. I stopped being muzungu and allowed myself to just be. I ate chapati and sukuma wiki with everyone

> As I learned more about all the different people, their languages and traditions and all the things that I could never really lay claim to, I became aware of the depth of the reward that comes when you agree to take a risk and believe in the miracle.

else. Since we often had no running water, I toted huge buckets of water like the women I had seen in the marketplace, but not nearly with that kind of grace. You become humble when you have to haul your bath water up four flights, and then heat it in an electric teakettle, pouring the water, kettle by kettle, into the tub. And after all that, you've still only managed to get enough tepid water to rinse off the sweat from climbing all those stairs, and then brush your teeth, before rushing out to morning classes.

Once the dorms moved from the far-off flats in Parklands onto the campus, we assumed we'd be living in the lap of luxury, comparatively speaking. Turns out that idea was completely wrong. We still sometimes had no running water. Only now we also periodically went without electricity. Like clockwork, the lights would go out the night before finals so that no one could study. I still think the maintenance men did it on purpose, just to laugh at the spoiled ex-pats and political brats. So, we would take our flashlights and trudge through the fields, where the boys used their machetes to behead the cobras, to the classroom bungalows to study there in groups.

We carried on with our studies, in spite of the howling of the insects and the eyes of the unnamed animals that roamed the fields with us, darting in and out of the light of our torches. With all its hardships, I was in love with this place. I knew exactly who I was here.

But then it all began to unravel.

While I'd been so blissfully lost in my cocoon, waking up to elephants outside the door of our manyatta in the highlands, and then coming home to hobnob with the children of kings and presidents and ambassadors at school, unrest had been building all along the borders. Every day the confluence of refugees in the streets, huddling in the alleys and on the corners, continued to grow. They were everywhere. We would go to town, my rich friends and I, to eat in restaurants or to shop and we'd see them: whole families sitting on cardboard boxes in the middle of the street, men looking like bones attached to sagging pieces of skin lying out on the sidewalk. I knew that it would be time to leave soon when I passed one of those men one day and looked down to realize that he was dead. The problem was not his death, but the fact that no one stopped, no one noticed. It felt too much like things I had seen at home.

People continued to come from all over. By now, I could tell the difference between the highland peoples and the Somali tribesmen, who'd been displaced from their homes along the border.

At first we didn't know exactly what was happening. There were so many ongoing conflicts, so many pieces unraveling. Then one night, we heard reports on the radio that the Rwandan president's plane had gone down. All the foreign students packed their bags immediately as we waited to hear more. Kenya was an extremely stable country, especially compared to the likes of Rwanda, but you could never tell with these things. We huddled in groups in front of the radio, because we knew that if anything "coincidentally" happened to President Moi, what was happening in Rwanda could easily spill across the border to where we were. Those who had the means to escape were prepared to do so at a moment's notice.

I waited with my heart in my throat, but not really understanding the import. Little by little, reports began to filter in about massacres across the border in Rwanda. People were being butchered. Even then, we didn't know the extent of what was happening. I actually didn't find out the truth until much later, after I had come home. Reports were sketchy and minimized. But what I did know was that my time on the continent was coming to a close. Life was changing, pushing me in a different direction. It was time for the miracle that I had been living to be replaced with something else. I'd given myself a year, and that year was up. It was time to chart the next part of the journey, though doing so caused me unspeakable sadness, not to mention guilt and fear for the people and places I was leaving behind.

Feeling more like a coward than I cared to admit, I flew home a few weeks later. I couldn't hold on to the moment, the beauty of belonging and the certainty of youth. But what I did hold on to was the truth of my heart: that I was an artist, a writer, whose words had meaning. I could share a voice and perspective that was different. Steinbeck's words had saved lives; I was sure of it. Zora Neale Hurston's words had changed lives; mine included. Baldwin brought jazz into stories were other people would only have heard the somber beat of a funeral march. If I could be like that, I reasoned, I could hold up the people I love so dearly with the strength of a thousand hands, rather than just my two. I could one day use words to help define my generation, as those others had done before me. I was determined to claim such a life as my own.

• • •

Fast-forward about fifteen years.

Life hadn't worked out exactly the way I thought it would. In fact, it hadn't worked out anything like I thought it would. It hadn't been bad, by any stretch of the imagination. It had actually been quite wonderful. It was just very, very different. These days, I often found myself questioning who I was, rather than boldly asserting who I intended to be and then giving the details over to Life as I walked on ahead.

How did that happen?

I recalled the dreams that I had had, that I now had to pull out and dust off. Could any of them be resurrected? Could any of it still be me? I didn't know. What did my current reality mean when faced with the dreams of the twenty-year-old girl I once was? And, more importantly, were her dreams even the same as those of a thirty-five-year-old woman? I didn't know. I had absently assumed that they were. But absent-minded assumptions have an annoying tendency to be wrong.

For example, I'd also assumed that maintaining a certain sense of balance would come naturally to me once my baby was born. I vividly remembered the women I knew in Kenya. In the marketplaces, in the shops, in the villages, the children were never far from the watchful eyes of their mother or some other female relative. The women shopped, sold their wares, bargained, and did all manner of other work without seeming to feel the need to separate or compartmentalize motherhood from the rest of their active lives.

I'd been imprinted by this idea without fully recognizing that in my own culture people actively propagated the belief that "motherhood" and "real life" were to be automatically relegated to two separate realms. Finding your elusive "work/life balance" had become a clichéd catchphrase that almost nobody, it seemed, knew how to master. People had bought into the idea that one's identity as a woman—a successful artist, a professional, a wife, a leader—would occupy a naturally conflicting space with one's identity as mother. To do one well, you'd naturally have to scrimp on the other.

This idea of living a compartmentalized life hadn't occurred to me because I'd seen how other people, with a different paradigm, lived in a reality where that wasn't necessarily the case. It shocked me how easy it was to fall into the same proscriptive patterns that felt so damaging and narrow. As a result, my days started to feel shorter and less productive, no matter how busy I became. I fell out of the flow that had come so naturally in the past. My miracles felt like they were drying up.

Somewhere along the way, probably long before my son

was born, I stopped seeing miracles as my birthright. Some-where along the way, I rounded up too many judgments about how things had to look, and how they should happen, and whether or not I was worthy or prepared to have and do the things that I wanted. I'd put so many limitations on the work-ings of an unlimited universe. Now I wanted to take them off and start again. If I were a child, I would just yell *Do over!* or *Psych!* and start again. Maybe that's why life could work so effortlessly for children.

• • •

Pulling myself mentally back to the present, I looked down at my son as we walked up the hill toward our home. He opened his eyes, stared up at me, and smiled. Joy spread through my body like a drop of paint across a canvas, and

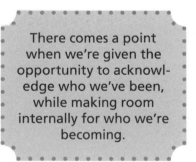

There comes a point when we're given the opportunity to acknowl-edge who we've been, while making room internally for who we're becoming.

I instantly had the answer to one of my questions: miracles were absolutely my birthright. They always had been and they always would be, whether I chose to see it and claim it or not. Every moment of my life was a miracle and Kingston was the biggest miracle of them all. I kissed the corners of the baby's mouth, smiling back, believing that somehow my new responsibilities would add to, rather than subtract from, the truth of my growing self.

There comes a point when we're given the opportunity to acknowledge who we've been, while making room internally for who we're becoming. I needed to make room, to make that forward move. It might change everything, I figured, but I had to try. As it turned out, everything was already about to change.

Help! I Look Like Somebody's Mother: Honoring the Body Temple

My cup runneth over. What comes out of the cup is for y'all. But what's in the cup is mine. I've got to keep my cup full.

—IYANLA VANZANT

I WOKE UP DRY-MOUTHED AND BARELY ABLE TO BREATHE. I refused to pull my head from underneath the pillow, where it was dark and cool. It felt like the worst hangover anyone could ever have. But it wasn't. It was just my birthday.

This was the year that I turned thirty-six. There was nothing innately wrong with thirty-six. It just felt heavy. Thirty-six felt like a very judgmental year, full of expectation. If I had been single and felt that way I probably wouldn't have gotten out of bed. I would've lounged under the covers until at least noon, then begrudgingly dressed for lunch at a Mexican restaurant somewhere in West Hollywood, where you're allowed to have margaritas that early.

This thirty-sixth year, I didn't have a choice. Babies don't know birthdays. Kingston was up at the crack of dawn, mewling and kicking his fat little legs beside me like he was pedaling a tiny, invisible bike. He cooed and called my name in his baby language, which sounded something like, *hiya mayay-aya ah ayaya!* This was his way of saying, *Mama, get up! I've got things to do today.* I nuzzled him and he rewarded me with a wide smile, showing off his nubby, pink gums. They were so beautiful, a perfect sight first thing in the morning, especially since I was working with this imaginary hangover.

I leaned in close to smell his milk breath. Babies smell like pure goodness. The joy of watching him enjoy the moment helped my head to clear. He was so perfect to me, so clearly and completely enough. I was working on being able to say the same about myself.

The wonderful thing about having a three-month-old baby is that they couldn't care less about your angst. Life needed to go on according to schedule, regardless of whether I was feeling sorry for myself on my birthday or not. So I crawled out of bed, wrapped him up in my arms, and we went about our business of getting dressed for the day.

Cory was already out the door on an early day. So the house was quiet, just Kingston and me. I changed the baby's diaper and pulled out a warm outfit that would keep him snug against the chill in the air—a little yellow shirt with brown long sleeves and a brown motorcycle on the front, a pair of heavy blue jeans with an elastic waistband to accommodate his fat belly, and his favorite pair of blue sneaker socks. The entire time, he cooed and fussed at me. He told jokes and then laughed at his own punch lines, which of course I couldn't understand. I washed his face and brushed his hair with his little white brush. Then, just to be sure, I brushed it again to get it to lie just so.

As much care and attention as I put into getting Kingston ready for the day I put as little into getting myself ready. I don't even know what I put on—probably some maternity jeans and one of an endless number of A-line pregnancy shirts, with my fuzzy gray sweater on top of it. That was my mommy uniform. I didn't feel bad about it at the time, because all the other mommies we passed on the street every day also had their own mommy uniform. It was like we were all soldiers enlisted in private armies, each with their own specific rules, regulations, and dress codes. The frumpier the better.

I had curled my shoulder-length hair the day before so that it would be pretty for my birthday. But then I didn't take the time to actually comb it. Instead, I just piled the whole thick mess up on top of my head and we walked out of the house.

We wound our way up through the hills, taking the backstreets toward church. I was very aware of the Los Angeles congestion on the main streets and I didn't want to subject Kingston to the smog and the exhaust from cars. So we never took the main street when we walked, always the residential streets winding through the hills.

It was a bright sunny day; crisp but not cold—the perfect December day in LA. Our neighborhood was silent except for the occasional barking dog or some cars or birds chirping. We walked leisurely beneath the tall palms and the peeling eucalyptus trees that dotted the yards, admiring the snow-capped mountains in the distance. The day was so clear, we could see all the way to Mount Baldy to the east. Kingston squeaked and wiggled in the carrier when he heard the squirrels in front of us chirping as they chased each other in circles up and down the trees. Self-pity aside, I couldn't have asked for a better day.

The homes in our neighborhood were a hodgepodge of styles, a Spanish-style here, a colonial there, a ranch house over here, a bungalow over there. Nothing matched or looked like it was in any kind of order, which was typical of Los Angeles. Everyone made their own individualized statement, stopping and putting down roots wherever they landed.

When we arrived at the church, we walked inside the bookstore to look around before heading over to see Cory in his office at the Prayer Ministry. The children's corner in the bookstore was a cozy nook stocked with books by people like Wayne Dyer, Neale Donald Walsh, and Toni Morrison. They were books for the self-actualized baby, full of positive energy and bright colors. Babies who shopped there tended to have very good chi.

I flashed the lively picture books in front of Kingston's face, but he couldn't have cared less. He was much more interested in eating the books than looking at them. Still, I pressed on. While looking for something I thought he might like a little better, I came across a book with a blue cover and pretty teenage girls on it. I picked it up and turned it over to see that it was a self-empowerment book for young women.

Oh, I thought. *This is great. I wish I'd seen books like this when I was a kid.*

As I leafed through, my eyes landed on a page where the author wrote, "You can be anything that you want to be! You can run a company if you want. You can choose to be a scientist or build robots, be an engineer or CEO. It used to be that women weren't given the option of being anything worthwhile. They were always expected to stay home and take care of babies. But nobody does that anymore!"

Kingston grabbed the book and started gnawing on the edge. I let him slobber on it for a few seconds before throwing it back on the shelf, facedown. What a slap in the face. What an unsubtle irony that this book, which clearly had a positive message and was meant to be empowering and inclusive, could be so thoughtlessly exclusive and disempowering because of poor language choice. Or maybe it wasn't just a few badly worded sentences. Maybe that was really how the author felt.

The little blue book reminded me anew that it was my birthday and I was depressed. I hurried out of the bookstore without buying anything, feeling angry. And undervalued. And unwanted. Stupid book.

Stupid insecurities.

I wondered if everybody secretly felt the same way about a woman who was not out there slaying dragons and being conspicuously impressive. And what about me? To be honest, did I secretly feel the same way? Did my mommy uniform render me invisible?

I'd been so concerned and preoccupied with, well, myself that I hadn't stopped to consider whether part of that navel gazing stemmed from some unspoken ambiguity inside my own mind. I knew for sure that I didn't want to be the type of person who could be so self-assured and overzealous that I was unable to value other ways of being that might be different from my own. I hoped I'd never been that person, but if I ever had been, I certainly wasn't anymore.

We walked through the parking lot and down the stairs toward the Agape South building where Cory worked, helping Rev. Kathleen run the Prayer Ministry and the Practitioner Core for the church. It was quite a job, organizing more than 400 practitioners and ministers, making sure everyone kept up with their daily, weekly, and monthly church responsibilities. As one of our minister friends put it, Cory's job was like herding kittens. Try getting 400 kittens on the same page and moving in the same direction at the same time. That's kind of a little bit impossible, no matter how spiritually enlightened those kittens might be.

But anyway, I walked down the wooden steps toward the south building, feeling the warm breeze and listening to the baby gurgle as he slapped my face with his pudgy fists. Again self-doubt was gently edged to the side as I was taken aback by the perfection of the moment. The truth was, there was nothing wrong with my world or any of the choices that I was making. Kuwana, the slayer of dragons, had taken a hiatus for a little while. The person filling in was equally loved and loving—in fact, even more so. So there shouldn't have been a problem. Unfortunately, *should* is the worst word in the English language. It's a rigid judgment word. Whenever the word *should* is used, it means that someone, somewhere has come up short.

In this case, I *should* have been wallowing in bliss like a pig in mud. Yet I was questioning. I *should* have been oozing contentment. Yet growing pains were making me cagey. The issue at hand had nothing to do with the fact that I'd chosen to take the time away from my own pursuits to be with my baby. But, rather, in the last few months I'd become more isolated, and, in that isolation, I'd begun to feel disconnected.

At a time when I most needed to be grounded in connection I'd allowed myself to drift. But of course I couldn't admit that. Disconnection, isolation, and doubt weren't feelings that I necessarily wanted to call attention to. But not acknowledging all facets of your truth is like walking around with an existential toupee perched on top of your head. Everyone can see the awkwardness of it but you. The knowing eyes of others may make you feel even more self-conscious, but you still don't want to just rip the damn thing off for fear of being truly exposed. No one wants to be exposed.

> Truth will find a way to be seen, no matter what you say or think about it.

The question is: do you want to take the risk anyway?

The answer to that question is: it doesn't matter. Truth will find a way to be seen, no matter what you say or think about it.

As Kingston and I walked past the windows of the other offices in the complex, I happened to catch a look at myself in the reflection of the window. It startled me. I saw this young woman with frizzy, pouffed-up hair and a shirt that didn't match her cargo pants, which didn't match the fuzzy sweater she was wearing, which didn't match the run-down sneakers. She was a hot mess. Her only saving grace was that she was carrying an absolutely adorable, well-dressed baby who looked like he belonged in a Target ad. That part made me smile. But when my eyes wandered back to her, I couldn't help but wonder, *What happened?*

To make matters worse, the mismatched woman was about fifteen pounds overweight. I sucked in my stomach (unfortunately, I couldn't suck in my butt) and kept walking. I tried to ignore myself, because I didn't know what else to do in that moment. I still wasn't ready to consciously acknowledge that anything felt wrong. It just seemed so ungrateful. Here I was with this beautiful, healthy, perfect baby, living in a beautiful home with a great husband and every opportunity in the world to move forward in my life in any way that I chose. Yet I felt devalued. I didn't recognize myself. At least, that was the tape that was playing in my mind. That's not what was actually happening. What was happening was that I was being called out of my comfort zone into a new way of being. And it was terrifying.

How could someone be so ridiculously happy and at the same time so frightened? Processing and expressing such stark contradictions would have felt overwhelming in that moment. Rather than dealing with the real questions of changing roles, identity, priorities, and goals, I glommed on to what I could see. Therefore, out of all that stuff, the only thought that I allowed myself to entertain was, *God, I have to start taking better care of myself. I need to lose some weight.*

Now, clearly, my outward appearance was a bright red indicator of what was going on inside. But it was a symptom of illness, not the cause. However, like a master of denial, I became convinced that all I needed was a good workout. I promised myself that I'd get up and go running the next day. Surely that would make it all better.

The next morning, bright and early at about 9:30 a.m., I threw on my pink sweatpants and a baggy T-shirt and laced up my ratty running shoes. I left Kingston with Cory and jumped into the car to make the five-minute trip up to the walk park nestled in the hills over our home. I felt good and powerful as I got out of the car, like I was doing something important for myself. Pushing the lock button on the key, I walked across the street toward the well-manicured track dotted with pine trees, yellow flowers, and the occasional fox trap. The day was overcast, so where the Hollywood sign would've been visible in the distance, there sat a cluster of clouds hugging the hillside.

This was going to be great. I was determined and focused. My iPhone was set to The Running Playlist. The weather was great—not too hot, not too cold. This was where I'd start the process of getting out of my rut. No more avoidance. It was time to (though I hated myself for thinking in clichés) *just do it.*

With purpose and passion I strode across the street. And just as I made it to the park's main entrance, the rain started. They were big, slow drops that came down harder and faster, even as I prayed it would be just a drizzle.

By the time I completed the first lap, the rain was pouring down and I was soaked to the bone. I looked around, conscious that I was the only person outside and that other people were driving past, staring at me like I was all kinds of crazy. In Los Angeles, everyone hides when it rains. As my grandpa used to say, they must think they're made of sugar and prone to melt in the rain. Angelenos and inclement weather do not mix, the standard definition of "inclement" being anything less than 68 degrees and partly sunny.

So I was all alone, just me, my iPhone, and the track. I went around and around, running until the cramps in my left calf begin to ease up. At the same time, the burning in my lungs got worse and worse, telling me to stop, to quit. I didn't. I wouldn't. I ran and ran until the pain was no longer painful. It was just part of me. *No matter what,* I thought, *I'm going to keep moving.*

With all of that, I still didn't go very far. I was ridiculously out of shape. But even though I'd barely made it three miles my energy had lifted. I felt stronger. The harder it rained, the faster I went. At the very end, I knew I was supposed to stop but I didn't want to. I wanted to keep going. I left the track, but instead of heading back to the car, I ran out and down the block toward the elementary school. Then I turned around and came back up the street. Three and a half miles accomplished.

By the time I reached the car, I felt exhausted but alive, like something in me was fired up again. Something was still able to push and to create and to do what I said I was going to do, and be what I said I was going to be. That thing inside me wasn't petrified by inactivity and self-pity. It was still there and waiting for me to acknowledge it and keep moving.

I drove back down through the hills, past the big beautiful homes on both sides of the street, across Slauson Avenue, and made a right onto our block. I pulled into our driveway feeling a little bit redeemed. Cory was waiting inside with the baby.

"Hey, beautiful. How did it go?" he asked.

"It went great," I replied. "I'm actually kind of proud of myself."

"You're soaked too," he said. "Go take a shower. I'll sit with the baby while you get dressed."

I grabbed something new to wear for the day and headed into the marble bathroom. As I slid into the shower and stood there under the water, washing away the rain and sweat, I felt even more invigorated.

Why had I waited so long to do something good for myself? What was wrong with me?

There's nothing wrong with you, the voice inside my head said. There's nothing wrong that a change in perception won't fix. You really are everything that you feel and think you are. You're simply asleep.

What was that supposed to mean? I hated it when my inner self talked to me in riddles. What exactly was I asleep to? If I was asleep, how could I shake myself awake?

> Life had shifted, like sand being pulled out from under my feet at high tide.

Cory gave the baby to me and headed out for a meeting. I carried Kingston back to his bedroom to get his clothes ready for the day. While I was dressing him, I once again caught sight of myself in the full-length mirror in front of my closet. Again I saw someone who was less familiar to me than the baby I was carrying in my arms. She was so much deeper than I remembered myself to be, so much more capable, yet not fully aware of the alteration in the balance of power within her own being.

When I'd looked at myself before, I'd only been seeing myself through the shallowest lens: the lens of emotional and physical insecurities. Life had shifted, like sand being pulled out from under my feet at high tide. Likewise, I had shifted into something new. The old foundation—so many of the things that I'd previously identified with—was getting swept out in the riptide.

I thought about how radically it would change my life if I accepted the notion that I'd been longing to be something that I already was. Somewhere along the way I'd chosen to believe a lesser vision that continued to exist regardless of any and all evidence to the contrary. All the internal drama had been the result of my choice to believe something other than the truth about me. But that was OK too. Inner discomfort, even chaos, is at the heart of emotional realignment; it brings forth the opportunity to make a new discovery, a better choice. That is the gift of the storm.

The great spiritual teacher Howard Thurman wrote a story about an old friend of his that seemed to perfectly fit this moment.

> When Lloyd George, the British statesman, was a boy, one of his family responsibilities was to collect firewood for warmth and for cooking. He discovered early that always, after a very terrific storm with high winds and driving rain, he had very little difficulty finding as much, and more, wood than he needed at the time.
>
> When the days were beautiful, sunny and the skies untroubled, firewood was at a premium. Despite the fact that the sunny days were happy ones for him, providing him with long hours to fill his heart with delight, nevertheless in terms of other needs, which were his specific responsibilities, they were his most difficult times.
>
> Many years after, he realized what had been happening. During the times of heavy rains and driving winds, many of the dead limbs were broken off and many rotten trees were toppled over. The living things were separated from the dead things. But when the sun was shining and the weather was clear and beautiful, the dead and the not dead were indistinguishable. The experience of Lloyd George is common to us all. When all is well with our

world, there is often no necessity to separate the dead from the not dead in our lives.

Under the pressure of crisis, when we need all available vitality, we are apt to discover that much in us is of no account, valueless… Given the storm, it is wisdom to know that when it comes the things that are firmly held by the vitality of life are apt to remain, chastened but confirmed. While the things that are dead, sterile, or lifeless are apt to be torn away.

Some things were being confirmed in my life while many, many other things were being torn away. And I was loath to let them go, even though I wasn't quite sure what those things were. The problem with change, what makes us uneasy about it, is that we never know where it's going to stop. I concluded that I would try my best to open up to what was being asked of me and to discover exactly what it was. What things of vitality were coming to the forefront, and what was being swept away in the wind?

Again the voice spoke into my questioning: The gift is in your knowing that no matter what happens, you are enough. When you start actually treating yourself as though you are enough, you'll see changes in your life that you could never have imagined. Treat yourself with the same reverence, respect, love, and kindness that you show your son and the world will open itself to you. You cannot have in this life what you are not willing to become. You cannot have what you are not willing to share. And in order to share anything with anyone, you must first share it with yourself.

> An awakened mind leans into the storm.

That idea sounded so simple, yet it felt so monumental. As the saying goes, simple and easy are two different things. I did want for myself all the same things I wanted for my son: a life of compassion and courage and risk taking, a life of fulfillment and joy. Embracing these qualities would mean mastering the skill of giving to myself. Otherwise how could I expect to be an effective guide, to show Kingston what it looked like to embrace passion and purpose? It's so easy to be punked by life, to allow life to take over and dictate the terms of your experience. The unconscious mind accepts the life that it's been given, and tries to find a dry space within those wet, chilly parameters to ride out the storms that are destined to come.

An awakened mind leans into the storm. It welcomes the challenge and change, and the pruning that occurs when the wind is at its fiercest. Every unnecessary thing is stripped away, leaving behind a conscious awareness of truth. No matter how painful or confusing it may be, the pruning is a gift. It has the power to awaken your passion for who you are and what you do every single moment of the day, no matter who you are or what you may be doing.

I Want It Now!: Surrendering Your Wants, Fulfilling Your Desires

Wash the dust from your soul and heart with wisdom's water.

—RUMI

DECEMBER WAS AN INCREDIBLY BUSY MONTH. THERE WERE
so many things that needed to be accomplished in such a short
period of time. I shook off my birthday blues, only to look
up and realize that the baby's christening was days away. I'd
planned a huge coming-out party for this three-month-old
boy without fully considering the fact that I was the one who
would have to pull the whole thing together. Oops.

We'd decided to hold the christening on December 13,
which was my grandfather's and my brother's birthday. I felt
that the date was appropriately significant, because it was
a symbol of the ties that bound the men on my side of the
family together. Also, Kingston's middle name was James,
in honor of my father, grandfather, and brother, all named
James. It just fit so perfectly. Besides, the 13th was the only
day that the church had available to do the christening. So we
pressed forward.

My mother was flying in all the way from New York for
the party. My cousin Roselyn, my oldest and dearest friend in
the world, was flying in from Oklahoma. Rosie was leaving
her husband and two children at home that weekend, because
she knew how much help I was going to need to pull everything together. Practically everyone we knew had agreed to

attend. Kingston didn't have godparents—he had a god-*village* of no less than nine people, all of whom were going to be in the ceremony with all their families. So we had to coordinate all these people, make sure they got to the church on time, got the reserved seating for the ceremony, and were able to get back to our house after the ceremony. We had to prepare food for everyone, and have sweets and games for the children. I was to orchestrate all of this while simultaneously handling the round-the-clock baby care that a three-month-old requires.

That seemed like it should've been enough. But, of course, there was more to come.

That Friday evening, I walked out the door and headed down our little sloping driveway to the car. Kingston fussed at me as I eased him into his car seat. But then, surprisingly, he calmed down and even smiled a little bit. Usually, he was a demon in the car seat. He couldn't stand being confined. On this particular day, however, he must've known that we were going to pick up Mama's favorite cousin. I slid behind the wheel and backed out of the driveway. We headed toward LAX, which was a ten-minute drive from our house.

We took the backstreets to avoid the rush-hour traffic, driving up La Tijera Boulevard, past the strip malls and apartment buildings. I was so excited about seeing Rosie again. It would feel so good to get a hug from someone who had known and loved me before, back in the old days. Back then, I was a knobby-kneed, sardonic child who rarely smiled for pictures and had an overdeveloped sense of the ironic. As one might imagine, I needed all the friends I could get.

When we approached the arrivals entrance outside the airport, I rolled down my window to feel the balmy airport air whip against my skin. The smell of jet fuel made me nostalgic. There was a time in my life when traveling to the airport meant that I'd be soon taking off to Amsterdam or South Africa for a few weeks to do some research for a book. Or maybe I'd be heading to Paris, just because.

I envisioned myself as I had been back then, notebook in hand, walking down narrow alleys of the red light district in Amsterdam as the bored-looking prostitutes sat in their windows, smoking cigarettes and waiting for their shift to be over. I recalled riding a broken-down green bicycle over the Herengracht Canal, seeing the narrow canal houses rising up on all sides of me, feeling hundreds of years' worth of history bumping under my feet. Then I saw myself jetting off to Tanzania, preparing to climb Kilimanjaro to see what was at the top of the world. I was going to write about it, to share such a personal adventure with people I'd never seen and would never see, and that had been life-changing.

In those times of confidence and triumph, I felt as though I had found a permanent way forward. Life was no match for me at my cleverest.

After a few years and a bit more experience I found myself in firm alignment with dear old Howard Thurmon, who wrote:

Little by little there crept into my life the dust and grit of the journey. Details, lower-level demands, all kinds of crosscurrents—nothing momentous, nothing overwhelming, nothing flagrant—just wear and tear...

In the quietness of this place surrounded by the all pervading presence of God, my heart whispers: Keep fresh before me the moments of my high resolve, that in fair weather or foul, in good times or tempests, in the days when the darkness and the foe are nameless or familiar, I may not forget that to which my life is committed.

The charge to remember that to which your life is committed, since well before you were born, is a fearsome undertaking. I'd been committed to many things, but maybe my real commitment went much further than even I knew. Beyond a shadow of a doubt, above all other things, I was committed to nurturing and protecting and raising our son. But there was something in addition to that, some reason that my soul had chosen to incarnate at this time, and I wanted to know what it was.

> The charge to remember that to which your life is committed, since well before you were born, is a fearsome undertaking.

No matter what my stir-crazy mind had been telling me, I wasn't committed to adventure. I may not even have been committed to art for the sake of art, in the way I envisioned it. The commitment was more fundamental than even that. But what then? The thought, the need to know, to figure it all out, wouldn't leave me alone.

Kingston and I fought our way through the arrivals traffic to the United Airlines terminal, checking for anybody standing outside who looked like they might hail from Oklahoma City. (Overalls? Gingham, perhaps? Forgive me, Rose.)

For a fleeting second I felt a little bit sad, a little landlocked. There would be no departures for us. Not today.

We were late as usual, rushing. I scanned the crowds trying to see Rosie's face. At first, I thought I was going to have to go around again, because some crazy-driving nut job cut me off at the last second, swerving into the pickup lane. I was sure I wouldn't be able to stop in time. LA drivers. But then I saw Rosie and veered into the pickup lane with a quick jerk of the wheel. I jumped out of the car and we squealed in unison. Everything that I'd been wrestling with melted away. That's the power of having one good friend.

"So! Where is that baby? I have to see him!" Rosie peeked into the backseat and said, "Oh! He's so beautiful. Hello, Kingston! Auntie is here. She's here to scoop you up and steal you from your mama!"

"You can borrow him," I corrected. "But you can't steal him. You have to bring him back or I'll have to come and catch you. Mommy won't let nobody steal her baby!"

Kingston giggled over the two crazy ladies fighting over him, holding up traffic in the airport pickup lane. We went back and forth until the people behind started honking at us. Rosie loaded her bags into the trunk and hopped into the backseat next to the baby as I took off toward Century Boulevard. We merged onto Century and then headed left onto La Cienega, where the traffic seemed to be a little lighter. Kingston hated to sit in traffic. He wanted movement.

"So what's going on?" Rosie asked. "How is everything?"

"It's going, I guess," I replied. "There's so much to do! Why is it that one party takes so much effort? I love entertaining. It didn't seem to be this hard before."

"That's because you didn't have this little pickle face to take care of before. You have to give him all your attention, don't you? He's so adorable! He's such a Haulsey. Look at that face!"

Kingston was delighted with the attention and milked it for all it was worth.

"Yes, he surely is a Haulsey," I agreed. "He's demanding and loud and he loves to talk. Don't you, Baby?"

Kingston babbled on in response. Whatever joke he had just told really cracked him up. Rosie and I were completely smitten with the sound of baby laughter. It sounded like pure love.

"Is your mom here yet?" Rosie asked.

"Yes," I said. "She got in last night and she's been driving me crazy ever since."

Rosie laughed. "She always drives you crazy, according to you."

"She wants everything to be perfect. And she has very specific ideas about what perfect looks like."

"Yeah, that sounds like a mom."

"Am I going to be that kind of mom?" I asked.

"No!" Rosie gasped. "Not you."

We both fell out into a fit of laughter.

As we made the turn onto our street, Rosie said, "So, has anything else been going on? You sounded a little down on the phone."

I wanted to answer her but the words were sticky, clinging to the back of my throat. I thought maybe if I could get them out, I might have a real good chance at wrestling this thing down. We were silent for a long minute.

Finally, I cleared my throat and said, "I'm okay. I'm just tired. There's so much going on and so much left to do. I really just need to learn to utilize my time better. I'm not very good at it yet."

"Yeah, that's hard, especially in the beginning. It's hard to gauge what needs to be done because things that used to take you twenty minutes can take two hours now sometimes. It seems like it shouldn't be that way, but it is. It gets much easier, though."

She looked at the baby. "Especially now that you're a little bit bigger. You're a big, strong strapping young man, aren't you? Aren't you, beautiful? You're making it easier for Mama. Pretty soon you'll be doing the dishes and sweeping the floor and helping Mama do all kinds of good chores.

Right? You'll be going to school and—"

"Hey, don't rush me!" I laughed. "I like him just the way he is. I get your point, though."

We pulled into the driveway of our little peach bungalow and turned off the car. I helped Rosie drag the bags from the trunk and then reached inside the car to grab the baby. He gurgled some more and nuzzled his nose into my neck as I held him up against my chest. Kingston turned his head to look at Rosie, and started talking and screaming all over again.

"I hear you, little man! That's some important news you have to share. Come into the house with Auntie and tell me more."

Rosie swooped the baby out of my arms and headed to the front door, which Cory was holding open for us.

"Hi, beautiful," he said, giving Rosie a kiss on the cheek. "Come on in and let me get those bags for you."

Cory looked at me and said, "Your mom is waiting for you inside."

I walked in behind Rosie and the baby, hearing my mother and my cousin laughing as they saw each other. They kissed and hugged as I dawdled behind, smiling. It felt so good to be walking into a warm, bright house, full of love. *This is what I want*, I thought. But as soon as I stepped inside, I remembered all the things that I still needed to do and say and decide and handle before I could sit down and socialize.

Usually, I loved party planning. It was one of my joys.

However, it can also be a quicksand trap where you get sucked down to your doom by overextension and ambition.

"So," Rosie said. "What are we doing tonight?"

"You're just going to relax and get some sleep," I told her.

"Okay, if you insist!" my mama chirped. "Thanks for offering. I'm still on New York time and I need my beauty sleep. But don't stay up too late. You know how grumpy you get when you don't have enough rest."

"*Ma*—"

"What do you need to do?" Rosie interrupted us.

"I'm going to start putting together the menu and shopping list and getting the supplies together."

Mommy yawned. "Wake me up if you need me to do anything."

Rosie caught me giving my mother the side eye and smiled at us.

"You know I'm staying up with you," she said.

I nodded. Rosie was going to help regardless of what I said, so I figured I might as well be gracious about it. A few minutes later, my mother and Kingston drifted off to sleep. In the quiet house, Rosie and I sat down in our theater of war and checked our battle plan. We needed to finalize the menu, compile all the recipes, set up a shopping list, make a shopping schedule, and decide when to pick up the tables and chairs from the party store. We were going to have balloons, which needed to match the silverware, which needed to match the plates. All of that had to be coordinated. I'd planned to make party favors too and was beside myself because it looked like there wouldn't be enough time to do it.

"Okay," Rosie said. "We're going to go through all of this and decide what's absolutely necessary and what can be let go of."

"But it's all necessary!" I argued. "I want it all. It's about the ambience. It's about creating an atmosphere. You take one thing away and the atmosphere is completely different. It's like having fog instead of sunshine. It makes it a totally different day."

Rosie sat patiently.

"Fine," I conceded. "But the one thing we absolutely have to do is make the cupcakes. I can't part with that."

"Okay," Rosie agreed. "The cupcakes are a necessity."

I'd obsessed over my homemade cupcake creations in the same way Shah Jahan must have obsessed over the minarets atop the Taj Mahal. Are they the right shape? The right color? Will they be able to catch the sun at the appropriate angles? That's where I was with these cupcakes. All my fire and passion and angst had been redirected to my safe place. If nothing else, I wanted simple, sweet, and safe for the next three days. Life could make its own plans after that. But I would be in charge of the next three days, and I was determined to have what I wanted.

Rosie and I stayed up most of the night talking, laughing, making menus, collecting napkins and plates, and calculating the exact number of balloons needed to indicate "festive" as opposed to "childlike." Looking around at the mayhem we were creating, I slid down onto the floor, pretending to pass out, and complained, "This is completely overwhelming."

"Yes," Rosie said brightly. "Sometimes you just need to let some things go and focus on what really matters."

Please! I thought, *Watch me do this.*

After a few hours' sleep, we were up bright and early, back to work. Sometime during the afternoon, my friend Xiomara appeared with a loud, purposeful knock on the door. Rosie swung both doors open wide. They laughed and hugged like they were the ones who were related. Then Xio turned to the baby.

"Hello, sweetheart," she sang, in her cheerful, crackly, completely off-key voice. "How are you? Yes, that's right! Yes! Tia is here! That's my godson. Did you know that, Rosie? Kingston is my godson."

"Yes," Rosie replied. "He's my godson too."

"See, there's something else we have in common," Xiomara replied magnanimously.

Xiomara held Kingston close and danced around the living room with the baby snuggled against her ample bosom. Kingston was delighted. Anytime he was in close proximity to large boobs, he was in his glory. I was still trying to explain to him that milk didn't come out of every pair of boobs, no matter how large, but he didn't get that concept quite yet. He drooled and happily smacked his lips, waiting for lunch to begin.

"So, what are we doing now?" Xiomara jumped into things as if she'd been there, working hard, the entire time. She wasn't the type of person who was familiar with beginnings. No matter what was going on, Xiomara always jumped right into the middle.

"When are we going to make the cupcakes?" she asked.

"I don't know, Xio," I admitted. "I... I just don't know how we're going have the time to make a hundred cupcakes from scratch. To tell you the truth, I was thinking about doing something awful."

"Such as..." Xiomara waited with her eyebrows furrowed.

I averted my eyes and mumbled, "Well, you know, I was thinking about using *a box mix*."

"What! What did you say?"

"A box mix! I said I wanted to use—"

"I heard you the first time. I have very good ears. A box cake? For *my* godson's christening? Ay, Díos! That's not acceptable. Kuwana, I'm little bit shocked."

I acknowledge that I am, at times, surrounded by cosigners on my perfectionist dysfunction. Birds of a feather, and all that.

"Yes, I know," I grumbled. "But there's just not enough time to do everything."

I glanced over at Rosie for support, but stopped just short

of saying the magic words: She was right. I bit off more than I could chew.

No matter. Xiomara was already reaching into the cabinets to pull down the flour. So, I strapped the baby onto my chest in his carrier and we got to work. We baked and boiled and stewed and sautéed for hours. The baby fell asleep and woke up, covered in flour. He fell asleep again, then woke up and nursed and slept and woke up. We were still working. He slept again for a few hours, and woke back up for a snack. Finally, he went down for the night.

After I eased him into bed, I went back into the kitchen to see what else still needed to be done. Mommy had tried to hang in there, but she fell asleep on the couch while sorting napkins by color. Meanwhile, Rosie, Xio, and I had finally gotten back to the cupcakes and were deep into the frosting side of things. Oreos and icing tips and Nilla wafers were everywhere.

Xio was making monkey faces, dotting on the bright, shiny eyes. In her infinite wisdom, she had decided to recycle the Oreo cookie cream, rather than using the #4 Bright White Wilton's Pen Frosting that I bought from Michael's Crafts specifically for this purpose. I looked over and gasped.

"Xio," I said, trying to sound reasonable. "We can't use this monkey."

"Why not?"

"What do you mean, why not? Look at him," I said. "The white frosting cream is full of chocolate cookie dust. The cupcake eyes are all cloudy now. That looks terrible."

Xio looked closer, examining the cupcake from various angles. "I don't see a problem."

"Xiomara," I said pointedly. "You can't see this? His eyes are bloodshot. He looks like he's been smoking weed."

"Well, everybody needs to relax a little," Xiomara said and laughed uproariously, her cackle ping-ponging off the walls and down the hallway.

I refused to crack a smile. Rather, I snatched up my butter knife and, with a flick of my wrist, eviscerated the offending monkey's eyes.

"This simply will not do," said I, the Hannibal Lecter of bakers.

"Fine." Xio grimaced, then leaned over and whispered to Rosie, "Somebody's getting a little uptight."

Maybe so.

Just then, the doorbell rang. I opened the security door, wondering who could be coming over at eleven o'clock at night.

"Hello, Mama."

Lo and behold, our friend Theresa and her boyfriend Deo stood on my front steps. I was shocked, because I hadn't seen Theresa in months, certainly not since the baby had been born.

"Hey!" I said, hugging her. "What are you doing here?"

"I just stopped by because Xio said that you'd probably need some clothes for the christening tomorrow and she asked me to bring over something nice."

Oh, really, Xio?

Theresa was the tall, beautiful spokesmodel in our group. She was the one with all the clothes and all the shoes and all the men. She had once shown up to one of our dinner parties with not one, not two, but three dates. We locked her out of the house and told her that she couldn't come in until she agreed to share some of those men with everybody else. If I were going to borrow clothes from anyone, it would be Theresa. Still, Xio had no right to launch a preemptive strike. It was my turn to give Xio the side eye.

"Don't you look at me like that!" Xio scolded. "Tell the truth. You have nothing to wear. The bad part is, you haven't even thought about the fact that you have nothing to wear. Because you know what? You don't ever think about yourself anymore. You think about everything else—the cupcakes, pasta salad, who's going to show up, who's not going to show up, the balloons, and the decorations. You're thinking about whether or not to put the baby in the adorable satin christening outfit that your mother and I picked out—which, by the way, you really should do, but that's neither here nor there. You're thinking about coordinating people, getting them directions, making sure they're there on time. You think about everything and everyone but yourself.

"I know you. And I knew that when you got to church and you were standing up on that stage in front of 1,500 people it would suddenly dawn on you that you looked like a bum. And you weren't going to like that. So, I took it upon myself to call Theresa. Sue me. We have to think about you for you. So that's what we did. You can be mad at me now if you want. I'm ready. Go."

Friends.

I was still trying to be angry, but I had to admit it was kind of fun to have us all together again. After I got married, and certainly after the baby came, we'd more or less gone separate ways. Though begrudging, I was kind of grateful too.

I picked a beautiful soft purple sweater and matching necklace and I promised to actually comb my hair in the morning when I got up.

Eventually Theresa and Deo left, while Xio and Rosie fell asleep sitting up on my sofa, their hands full of party favors. By about three or four in the morning, even my eyes were closing against my will. There was still so much to do, but it would have to wait. I staggered down the hall and into the bedroom. I had just enough energy to strip my clothes off and climb into bed. As soon as I did, Kingston started rooting around in the darkness, smacking his lips. Even though I couldn't see him I could tell that he was giving me the milk face. I was so tired I could've cried.

"Okay," I sighed. "Milk for you."

I pulled him close and smelled the intoxicating smell of milk and new skin. It melted the tiredness out of my heart, leaving a warm, soft glow behind, as he molded his body against mine and nursed. He looked up at me with sleepy eyes and we watched each other quietly in the dark. I was so in touch with his needs. Often, I would wake up seconds before he did during the night and wait for him to purse his little lips and start rooting in the darkness for my breast. Then I'd snuggle him close and he would nurse without ever waking up.

I could read his face and tell when he was about to need a clean diaper, so I'd get one ready. When it was time to play, he'd stare at me until I met his gaze, then he'd smile and kick until I stopped what I was doing, magnetized to his joy. Perhaps I was so in touch with his needs partly because he was so in touch with all of his needs. He was clear. By watching him and focusing on his clarity, I had the opportunity to become clear too. Each time one of his desires was fulfilled, he instantaneously moved forward into the next moment. He experienced peace in his immediacy, not panic or expectation or overwhelm.

I was so focused on what I wanted to do, what I wanted to accomplish, what I wanted people to think or perceive about me. But I was aware of so little about what was truly moving me, what was operating behind my desires. To be continually in a state of wanting or needing something that I felt I didn't have just primed me to experience more lack—lack of time, energy, clarity, or resources. To be in touch with my desires, on the other hand, created a sense of excitement, the anticipation of fulfillment.

> By watching him and focusing on his clarity, I had the opportunity to become clear too.

Kingston never questioned whether or not I would respond to him. It was a given. I had the option of allowing life to respond to me with the same tenderness and devotion, if I'd let it. I needed to get back in touch with the desires of my spirit, to commit to being the person I was meant to be.

Three and a half hours later, it was time to get up. I was still rushed. But I was also able to take the time, even if just for a few seconds, to be present with myself.

As we stood on the stage in front of 1,500 people, holding our baby with our village surrounding us, I decided to let go of the fact that so many of my plans remained undone. I decided to be OK with things being incomplete, and enjoy the moment of celebration and connection that had been laid out so brilliantly before us. It wasn't an easy decision for me to make. But I did it. It was a step.

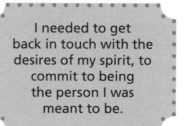

I needed to get back in touch with the desires of my spirit, to commit to being the person I was meant to be.

When It All Falls Apart: The Art of Joyous Failure

There is only time enough to iron your cape...
and back to the skies for you.

—JASON HARLEY

Before the beginning of great brilliance, there
must be chaos.

—SUPER K FORTUNE COOKIE

THE WEEKEND ENDED, AND I STILL DIDN'T GET EVERYTHING done that I wanted to get done. There was chaos, mayhem, uncooked food, and lopsided cupcakes. Everything that I swore would not happen, happened. Yet and still, everyone had a beautiful time. They all came together to celebrate the baby and the fact that we had been brought close, as a sacred circle of people who were blessed to be in this place, at this moment. We'd forged new bonds as we celebrated the life, recognizing the connection that comes with being part of a village steeped in love and mutual respect.

I was beginning to see how it was possible to create a totally different energy in my life by placing my attention on what was real, as opposed to what I *hoped* would be real or other people's perception of what was real for me. I was even starting to let go of the attachment to *my* perception of me. Learning to see something new about myself required me to see beyond my own perceptions, whether good or bad, and know that I was always bigger than I appeared to be in any one moment in time. Particularly when the moment included cupcake meltdowns and tantrums (mine, not Kingston's).

Things wound down and got much quieter over the next few days. My mother went home on Monday morning and

Rosie went home on Monday night. Xio disappeared again, as quickly as she'd come. We hadn't really been close like we used to be after I got married, and certainly after the baby had come. But it was good to see her again. It made me happy.

And so, by Tuesday, it was back to what I had grown accustomed to over the last few months—me and the baby in the house, just us. The only remnant of all the activity and the noise and the chatter and the people was the mess that was left behind. The house needed to be cleaned.

Kingston wasn't the kind of baby you could lay down in a bouncy seat or bassinet for any period of time. He insisted on being up, active, and doing whatever I was doing. So I strapped him to my chest and, together, we went about cleaning up the crap. We swept, washed, rinsed, scraped, and gathered, working to get everything back into some semblance of order. As we worked, with Kingston cooing in my ear and pulling on my hair, I began to have fun. I liked the order. I liked getting things to a place where I felt free and clean. I wanted that feeling of starting anew to last.

It had been three and a half months since Kingston had shown up in our lives, and I felt like I was ready to take some of what I was learning about him, and about us together, and put that information to use. For as long as I could remember, whenever life had given me material to use, I gladly repurposed it in my art. It was time to start transferring some of what I was learning back onto the page. My mind immediately went to my novel, my third book, which had been sitting unfinished on my desktop for nearly a year. Now was as good a time as any to finish it.

> When left alone to flow freely, this creativity became a wellspring of joy and light.

As we neared the end of the cleanup, I began to get excited. This was something I could complete and be proud of. It was something I could show our son when he was old enough. I'd let him know that, in the most fundamental way, I'd written it for him.

In my novel, a mother had to choose between saving the life of one child over another. She's haunted by the choice that she makes, which changes everything about the rest of their lives forever. It was a novel about choice and freedom, about discovering who one is in the midst of the hardships and trials of life, rather than in the light of their absence. It was a beautiful story, if I do say so myself, but one that had never seen the light of day. That always bothered me. It felt like a personal or moral failing that I hadn't been able to get it done faster and better.

Now, with Kingston here, I realized I'd been trying to write about something that I hadn't known anything about: the unspeakable choices of motherhood. No wonder it felt so difficult for me to do it convincingly. But now would be the time. I wanted to give myself over to the creative impulse that had birthed my baby and made life worth living. It was the same impulse that allowed me to grow from a girl who

> I would rise above complacency, quelling the little voice in my head that wanted to sweet-talk me into staying right where I was.

thought she knew everything into a woman who knew she didn't know much of anything, but at least had the courage to ask some compelling questions. When left alone to flow freely, this creativity became a wellspring of joy and light. It was the written representation of grace. When I didn't allow it to come freely, life felt constricted. It was painful.

In addition to loving my son, creating stories was something I felt called to do, another reason why I was here on the planet. In my mind, my willingness to walk this path had a lot to do with the reason Kingston had chosen to come through me. There was something in me to be shared with the spirit of imagination and creativity inside him.

I wanted to show Kingston what it looked like to live from truth. I wanted him to be accustomed to moving through life from a place of power and authenticity. So, I needed to create. It was just that simple.

The more I thought about it, the more intricate my ideas became. I'd be able to write about all the deep things, the messy things, that make life worth living. I'd be able to fight my fear of the unknown through the exploration of my hero's journey. Winning in this way would mean that I'd lived up to an internal barometer of excellence, an image of worth and value that came from doing what I set out to do. No excuses.

I would rise above complacency, quelling the little voice in my head that wanted to sweet-talk me into staying right where I was.

In the evening, when Cory got home from Agape, I was at the door, ready and waiting to talk to him. He came in and sat down at the dining table. Collapsed is a more accurate word, he was so tired. After sitting there for a second, he looked over at me, smiled, and held his arms out for the baby.

"Hey, you guys," he said. "How was your day today? What did you do?"

"Oh, you know, a little of this, a little of that. Went jogging, shot some pool, the usual."

Kingston bounced his legs up and down on his daddy's lap while he leaned forward and pounded Cory's nose, smiling and drooling. Then he nuzzled his face into his daddy's neck.

"Do we have anything to eat?" Cory asked. "I'm starving."

"I'll fix dinner now that you're here. But, um, actually I'd like to talk to you about something else."

I could see him tense up.

"Oh, really? What?" He tried looking nonchalant.

"Well, I've been thinking. I want to start back on my book again."

"Really! Is that it?" He relaxed visibly. "I think that's a great idea. How can I help? What can I do?"

I smiled. "Well, there's really nothing you can do. Okay, that's not true. There is something you can do. I'm going to need help with the baby so that I have the time to work out this story."

"I can do that! That's not a problem. How much time do you need? I know you're a night owl. But, you know, that doesn't work too well anymore. So maybe we can start your workday at five a.m., bright and early before Kingston wakes up. What do you think of that? You can just get up with me at five and I'll listen out for the baby while you get to work. Yes, that's a plan—"

Off to the races he went. I couldn't get a word in edgewise. Part of me was excited that he was so excited. But another part of me was all nerves. This was about more than just completing a book, which I'd done before numerous times. For me, this was about turning a corner.

"Don't worry," I said. "I'll figure it out. Thanks for the suggestions, though. Right now, I just need you to be open to being here with me and the baby. That's all."

"Are you sure? Because I could—"

"Yes, I'm sure. Believe me. I don't need anything else at this moment. I'll let you know when I do."

"Okay, we can start right now," Cory said, picking up the baby. "Come with Daddy into the backyard and tell me about your day while Mama makes some dinner. And after she finishes cooking she can get to work and we'll head out on an adventure. Maybe we'll go for walk. What do you think, little man?"

"Isn't it getting a little too chilly?"

"No, he loves it. Don't you, Bubby?"

Kingston squealed at the top of his lungs for emphasis.

As Cory took the baby in the back, I pulled out my pots and pans and put them on the stove. I wasn't even sure what to make for dinner, much less how to restructure a 300-page novel. But I figured something would jump out at me in both cases. There would be something in the cabinets, or the refrigerator, or the pantry, just like there'd have to be something stored way in the back of my mind, something that I could pull out and set down on the page. I hoped.

I took some fish out of the freezer and some broccoli from the refrigerator and chopped zucchini and onions to go with it. Maybe I could put on a little bit of rice. Before I knew it, the kitchen smelled really good. I could hear Cory chuckling from the back of the house and the baby squealing. I could picture his soft, warm body wiggling with delight.

Kingston's crying bouts had lessened a lot since he got over his colic hump. Now I didn't feel as though I was holding him in a blanket of eggshells and if I made one wrong move, something would break. I could breathe again.

Pretty soon dinner was done. Cory brought the baby out to the dining room while I dished up the food. I tried to eat with one hand while I cradled Kingston with the other. He couldn't eat solid food yet but he loved to grab for it and talk to it. He tried to cajole the food to float across the plate, toward his open mouth.

"No, no, no little one," I told him. "You have to wait.

That food is not for you. You have to wait until you grow some teeth. When you have some new teeth, then you can have some new food. That's the deal."

Kingston scowled at me, clearly unhappy.

Once the dinner was done and the food was put away, Cory bundled the baby up and strapped him into his carrier. They headed up the street to the drugstore. I had about an hour or so before Cory would be back with the baby for bedtime.

"I know it's not a lot of time to start with, but it's something," he said.

"Thank you." I kissed his forehead. "I appreciate it."

With that, they walked out the door. I carried my laptop over to the table, sat down, and opened it up. Immediately, my eyes begin to wander. I tried again to focus and I did: on a big, gooey, fishy food stain sitting right in the middle of my pretty rosewood table. I looked a little closer and saw crumbs and grains of rice everywhere. Even worse, there was another stain that looked like tomatoes. We didn't eat anything with tomatoes tonight. Could that dried-up food stain have been from yesterday? Egads!

Frustrated, I closed the computer, put it down on the chair, and strode into the kitchen. *I can't work in a space that smells like fish. That's ridiculous.*

The table got a thorough spritzing with my organic cleaner and then a hard scrub. I looked at it from above. Clean. Then I bent down to check it out from eye level. Crumbs. I whipped out my cleaner and dishrag again. After another scrub, the wood fairly sparkled. Just to be sure, I squatted down to check my handiwork from a different angle. Finally, it was clean. But now I had to wait for the table to dry. I couldn't put the computer on the wet table, could I?

While the table was drying, I figured I might as well make some tea. So I set the computer on the counter and grabbed my teapot. By the time I came back, the table was mostly dry. I felt confident about putting my computer down. But, just in case, I grabbed a paper towel from the counter and did a dry wipe.

I flicked the laptop open, pulled up my file, and scanned the pages inside. *Where exactly was I going with this?*

What had been so important to me the last time I sat down to write? The characters were still there, exactly where I'd left them, waiting for their expansion:

> For a long time, the two girls played venturing games at the river's edge, toes in, feet out, boldly daring the water to overrun its banks and come forward, whispering close. The river played coy. It was unyielding, unconcerned. It yawned a distracted wind into their faces. So the girls began to tease the water, to walk across it, skipping gingerly from rock to rock. They kneeled and pressed their lips against the water's face, murmuring secrets. Charmed, finally, the river spoke back. Billie heard it, clear as day, and after she heard it, Emma did too. The girls listened closely to its gentle hum and began repeating what they

heard; they told essential creation stories using the river's voice, happily sculpting new worlds for themselves out of the wet clay of the old one.

Their mother Madeline watched from close by as the sky turned a drunken, careless blue, its color so full that it overflowed the horizon and spilled across the mountaintops above their heads. Lake Isabella lay a few miles behind them, dammed, turquoise, as still as stained glass. The Kern River rolled beside, cold and pale gray, robbed of its color by restless motion, banked high and low by a riot of wildflowers. Purple monkshood, pussytoes, Indian hemp, fairy lanterns, fuzz-covered wild ginger, and mariposa lilies smeared the ground with their astonishing paint.

The teapot began to scream, loud and insistent as a train whistle. Tea's ready. So I went to the kitchen to fix myself a nice cup. Then, with my hot tea in hand, I sat back down. *You know what needs to go with this tea? A piece of that chocolate cake I made the other day. That would be perfect.* I got back up again and went to the kitchen for plates and knife. This back-and-forth went on for quite some time.

By the time Cory and Kingston returned from their walk, I hadn't written a single new word.

"How's it going?" Cory asked excitedly as he opened the door.

The baby smiled as he saw my face, his bright red cheeks looking like tight, shiny apples. His little nose was running a bit and I jumped up for a tissue to wipe it.

"Look at this little baby's nose. That's okay. Mama can fix it," I crooned as the baby tried to swipe my hand away.

"Hey, did you hear me?" Cory asked again. "How's it going?"

"Oh, you know, it's going. It feels a little rusty, but it's going," I lied.

"Well, it'll get easier," he said. "We'll be in the bedroom. I think somebody needs a new diaper."

They walked away and I sat back down at the computer. Again. You can do this, I told myself. This is what you do. You've been doing it forever. You teach other people how to do this. You can do this. It's not hard.

Somehow I still wasn't doing it. I didn't even know how to begin to do it.

My mind started wandering. Again. I thought about the books that I'd ghostwritten for other people. For the last few years I'd allowed myself to become professionally invisible, letting others benefit from whatever my words had to offer. I didn't claim any of the good stuff for myself. I thought back to one of the last things I'd published under my own name. I had to do some long-range thinking, all the way back to a trip that we took to Tanzania two years before, right before Cory and I officially got engaged.

• • •

I'd written a magazine article about our trek up Mount Kilimanjaro. Climbing Kilimanjaro had been a goal of mine for thirteen years, since I'd first lived in Africa. When Cory and I arrived at the foot of Kilimanjaro, I was ready to fulfill that ambition. I'd lived with the dream for so long that it never even occurred to me that I could fail to make the summit.

Cory and I and our guide, Boniface, climbed through every vegetation zone in five days—the jungle, the highlands, the desert, the moorlands, and, finally, up into the glaciers. On the second night, I stood at the mountain's edge with the clouds washing against the rocks at my feet, like the roiling white foam of a crashing ocean. Tilting my head back, I saw a network of stars—so many, in fact, that they appeared to be getting squeezed out of the heavens. One after another, shooting stars flashed across the sky toward the earth. Being born and raised a Bronx girl, I'd never seen anything like that before in my life. It stunned and humbled me. Everything looked as distinct as daytime, just different.

We started our final push for the summit at midnight. I stepped out under that canopy of stars and breathed in the frigid air, with the glaciers hanging above me. I knew that this was a life I had been born to live. I was an adventurer. What a magnificent job title.

That night, we walked and walked and walked. As the hours wore on and the altitude sickness began to set in, I got weaker and woozier. I walked and climbed and fell and got up and walked again and fell again. Rocks and gravel dug into my palms every time I hit the ground. My eyes got heavy and my vision strained as I fought to get back up each time. But I refused to give up. I couldn't fail at something so important.

Holding my walking stick like a staff, I moved straight ahead, concentrating on the path in front of me. I had to keep going. I had to make it. This was my one shot to do what I had dreamed of doing for so long. I wasn't going to give up.

But then, two hours before we reached the first summit, I started throwing up. I lost my balance and fell down for the last time. That was it.

I failed.

The only thing I could tell myself as consolation was, *Well, this will make for one hell of a magazine article.* And it did. It was a beautiful piece. I can imagine that it almost didn't matter to the people who read it that I had actually failed to achieve my goal. From the feedback I got, that little detail didn't seem to register with too many people besides myself. Readers were too engrossed in the beauty and the harshness of the climb. I wasn't quite so kind: I didn't make it. Period. My personal concept of failure was that there shouldn't be any. You don't step onto the court unless you intend to win, and all that.

• • •

My mind snapped back to the present and to my current challenge. Would I really be able to accomplish the writing of this book? Or would I blow it? This book was as big an undertaking as climbing a mountain, and just as dangerous. All of a sudden, I didn't know.

"I guess the only thing you can do," I mumbled under my breath, "is try."

My fingers hovered over the keys as I waited for the words to appear behind my eyes. Then I could start to type:

This is the reactive phase where the bone breaks and the water spills directly from the bone, from the dark gray marrow, hemorrhaging in waves with a wicked, seeping undertow.

This is where I got lost.

Let me start over.

This is the hardest story to tell because the voices all run together. They're merged, married in the way of running water when it swoons and couples, river to ocean. Bodies converge and can never again be undone. They create byways and they create gulfs, yet they are one. The appearance of separation may at times be quite convincing, but anyone who has faced water with no shore knows the truth.

There is no separation.

Sand to stone, ocean to ocean, blood to bone, mother to child: life is a permeable substance, a fluid grace. It can appear, to the uninitiated, to be many different things, each set apart from the other. Of course, that's not really true.

In the same way, these voices might appear to be three separate people. But in my arrogance, I don't believe that and it makes me unsure how to begin.

I don't know which voice is mine.

Wasn't that the truth.

Which voice was mine? What was I trying to say? More words were there, just out of reach. Slowly, teasingly, they began to come closer. I could barely breathe as I listened, waiting. And then... And then...

"Waaaaahhh! Waaaahhh!"

The screaming got louder as Cory walked the baby down the hall toward the dining room.

"Sorry," he said with a sheepish smile. "He doesn't want me anymore. He wants you and the milk."

"Right now? Can't you walk him or something?"

"I've done that already. I don't know what else to do. He's not cooperating."

Kingston was red-faced and sniffling, leaning his body out toward me. His eyes met mine and, just like that, the words were forgotten.

I closed the computer and went to my son. As soon as he was snuggled into my arms, he stopped screaming and started to hiccup.

"All right. All right, Mr. Baby." I hugged him tight as we walked over to the couch. "Come with me a little while. Step into my office. It's not that bad. Mommy's right here with you, my sweet love. Let's have some milk."

That's how it started and how it continued, day after day. For the next few weeks, every time I sat down to write, something came up. The baby needed something or Cory was hungry or somebody would call or I just couldn't do it. I felt like ripping my hair out strand by strand. It wasn't just a failure—it was a crash and burn.

It was like I was reaching with everything I had to make it up those last 2,000 feet of mountainside, but no matter

> Success doesn't exist without failure, without contrast.

what I did, I kept sliding backward. What had changed in me? I didn't want my son to grow up knowing his mother was a failure, someone who was unable to accomplish the big goals she set for herself. Yet here I was struggling day after day to do something that I clearly knew how to do. I just wasn't making it happen. In my heart, I believed that failure was synonymous with flaws and judgment and criticism. Somebody had to win at life, and if it wasn't you, there was probably a good reason. It was too hard to accept the parts of myself that, in my mind, didn't measure up.

Then, one afternoon, Kingston and I were lying on the floor. He was playing on his gym mat, swiping at the little monkeys and lions hanging just out of his reach. And he could catch nary a one of them. He'd stop to wiggle his fingers in front of his face, studying them as if he were trying to maneuver a foreign object. Then he'd swipe again. I could've watched him all day. Then it hit me—like a smack on the forehead.

Success doesn't exist without failure, without contrast. Achieving or not achieving a goal has nothing to do with personal worth—it has everything to do with the willingness to grow. As Rev. Michael once told me, "Be grateful to receive all that you require to wake up." Failure is a requirement. It's vital to the journey because it breaks open our psychological and emotional illusions so that we can wake up. In the larger sense, there's no such thing as failure. My son wasn't failing because he didn't have the motor skills to hit the plushy toy. He was, at every moment, in the process of developing new skills, while simultaneously deepening his mastery of other skills.

I had a choice to court the awareness that I was already succeeding in a much greater goal by staying flexible and open to growth. Kingston, with his constant demands, was helping me shift into that perspective. My real task was to learn to stop chasing after things that I wanted, and start accepting and receiving what I actually needed to wake up.

Yielding to the Divine Creative Within

Galaxies emerged out of the primordial silence, from which all creation flows. You and I are made out of that sacred image. Our lives, and the galaxies that we spin, break out of nothing but an idea, an inner pattern of good, if we will but contemplate it.

—MICHAEL BERNARD BECKWITH

THE WEEKS PASSED AND THE RAINY SEASON CAME DOWN hard, much harder than I'd become accustomed to over the past few years. This was good for the city, which seemed to be in a perpetual fear of drought, but difficult for us. There were days when the rain didn't seem to want to let up. It gushed down from the hills in sheets, creating wide, shallow lakes that stretched from one side of the street to the other. The water rolled down from our terraced backyard and seeped under the French doors into the bedroom to soak the thick carpets.

Normally, I loved the rain. It had a moody presence, like the weather back home in New York. I missed watching the seasons change. Seasons change in LA, but so subtly. When the leaves fall, they do it silently. New York leaves are loud, riotous in their color. They are bold and attitudinal and frisky. New York weather gets up in your face. The seasons in LA, by contrast, are demure and well coiffed. On the three days a year when it does rain, the city looks like Audrey Hepburn in the climactic scene of *Breakfast at Tiffany's*: helpless and disheveled, but artfully so.

Rainy days in LA are usually a rare and unexpected treat. The energy becomes new, not to mention the air quality. But this year, being stuck in the house with a fidgety baby took some of the excitement out of it for us. Kingston and I were both getting cabin fever in a big way. We sang and listened to music and did tummy time—and then what? My only saving grace was that the rain fascinated Kingston. So I wrapped us both up tight in a fluffy tan blanket, and we sat at the door, opened just a crack.

It amazed me to watch him watch the water falling from the sky like magic. He gasped as fat raindrops dropped down from the top of the doorframe onto the welcome mat at our feet. He'd swipe at the drops as they fell, not quick enough to catch any, but never discouraged. It was so much fun watching him scheme on those raindrops. He had no concept of judgment or impatience with this new game. Every time he grabbed for a raindrop and missed was one step closer to getting his timing just right.

By the end of January, going into February, I needed a change to brighten up the monotony that had set in. Kingston had just turned five months old and he was glorious. He was already sitting by himself for the most part. When he toppled over, he'd laugh and roll onto his back to immediately attempt this magic sitting posture again.

Over the last few months, he'd grown so deliciously fat that it was hard not to scoop him up and eat him. The rolls of fat on Kingston's legs looked like melting ice cream on a sundae. He had a triple chin and a smile that spread from the center of his being and shot out straight through his eyes. He just glowed, my little golden boy. His honey skin had undertones of strawberries and cream and the wild, curly black hair was starting to lighten up, giving way to a sandy brown color with blond highlights. He was so beautiful it hurt. I'd watch him and try to figure out what I could do to make him laugh so I could see his toothless, sloppy, glorious expression. He put his whole body into his smiles. Watching him smile like he did when it rained were some of the happiest moments of my life thus far.

On a Tuesday evening, as we sat in our spot in the doorway, I saw the lights of our car heading down the hill toward our house.

"Look, Baby, there's Daddy. Daddy's home from work. Yay!"

Cory turned into the driveway and coasted up the short incline. He jumped out of the car and ran to the front door, kissing us both hello as he slipped inside.

"Daddy's home and he's got good news."

"What is it?" I asked. "We need some good news in this house."

I thought about my book, which had been sitting untouched for the last three days. Every time the book popped into my mind, I saw myself slowly sliding off the side of the mountain. Yes, good news was definitely in order.

"You and I are going to be manifesters."

"Manifesters? Really? What exactly are we supposed to be manifesting?"

"What do you want to manifest?" he asked, with a big grin.

My husband is interesting. He's *so* LA, and I'm *so* Story Avenue in the Bronx. Most of the time we meet in the middle. Most of the time.

"Let's try again. What are you talking about?"

"Well, we've just been invited to take a teleseminar with Kathryn Alice."

He was referring to the author, speaker, love guru, and Agape practitioner. So far, he'd said the right thing to pique my interest. Kathryn Alice was awesome.

"What's this course about?"

"It's called Deliberate Creation," Cory said, swiping his hand across the air in front of my face.

"And how much are we deliberately paying for this seminar?" I asked.

"Only a hundred dollars," he said quickly. "And that covers four whole weeks."

"Maybe the first thing we should manifest is the money to pay ourselves back."

"Yes, we will," Cory said. "I bet we can manifest a lot more than that."

As impractical as my husband can be, he can be pretty cute when he's excited. I decided to take the bait.

"So what, exactly, are we trying to manifest here?"

"Your heart's desire," he said vaguely.

I looked at Kingston. "Mama thinks that Daddy has something up his sleeve, baby. What do you think?"

"I don't have anything up my sleeve," Cory said innocently. "I really think this is a good idea. We've both been stuck in the house for the last few months. We need to do something fun to jump-start our imagination. So I figured, why not?"

"Okay. Fine. When does it start?"

"Tonight! We just turn on the computer and go online at eight o'clock and listen in. That's it. And make our list. But that's it."

"What list?"

"List of things we want to manifest during the course of the course."

"What if I don't know what I want to manifest?"

"Well, that would be a problem. You can't get anywhere if you don't know where you're going. Maybe we should think about that. What exactly do we want? Let's assume that we can do anything. But we have to know what that anything is."

Suddenly, I didn't know whether I wanted to scream or laugh. Cory had very innocently hit on something of tremendous importance. What did I want to do? If I was open and able to do anything, what would that "anything" look like? How would "anything" make me feel? What was it about "anything" that would make my heart leap, the way it did when I sometimes turned around and caught sight of the baby's face in an unexpected moment? My breath would get caught in the back of my throat and everything in the world seemed just a little bit lighter. Was there anything in the outside world that could give me a feeling like that? I didn't know. But I surely did hope so. I would've been happy if anything even came close to that.

Kingston knew exactly what he liked and exactly what he wanted from his world. I could tell by the sheer joy that radiated from him when he caught sight of something or someone that was his beloved, including myself. He also very clearly knew what he didn't like, but those things didn't elicit the same sort of reaction from him. He seemed so effortless in his enthusiasm. Sometimes I felt like I was the exact opposite. I knew more about what I *didn't* like and what I *didn't* want than what I did. For example, I thought to myself, *Did I really want to finish my book, or did I just* not *want to fail?* These were two completely different things.

"Let's think about it," Cory offered. "Let's brainstorm. What's on your list?"

"Well," I said, immediately putting up my sarcasm shield, "I'd like to manifest a new Benz. I don't like ours anymore. I want a new, red one. I've always wanted a red convertible. The car that we have is so 2006. And silver? Everybody's done it. Red makes a statement. No! Wait! Lavender. Picture it, a convertible lavender Benz."

Cory shook his head, took the baby from me, and started walking into the kitchen.

"Make all the jokes you want," Cory said. "I don't know about you, but I'm going to make the most of this."

I played contrite. "All right. I'll start taking my magic a little more seriously. What do you want to manifest?"

"I'd like to manifest a new home for us."

"I like that manifestation," I said. "I can get on board with that." The place where we lived was gorgeous, but it wasn't ours. The owner hadn't been willing to sell to us for a decent price. In fact, the price he quoted was about double our budget. So we rented the property instead. But deep down, both of us would have preferred to own it. That way, no matter what, we'd have somewhere to put down roots. I wanted somewhere that Kingston would always be able to come back home to, something that we'd be able to pass down to him. I'd never before thought that far into the future, unless I was imagining myself as a silver-haired matriarch accepting my second or third Pulitzer Prize.

In those daydreams, I always saw myself in a smart, cream-colored suit, with a plunging neck and a lacy white camisole underneath, to maintain a healthy level of propriety. I wore high-heeled, camel-colored pumps with long, wild hair and flirty jewelry. I'd take the stage to speak about the craft of writing and the beauty and necessity of imagination. Then I'd thank all of the people in my life who supported me and helped push me toward yet another Pulitzer. Kingston and Cory and my mother would be seated in the front row, tears in their eyes, applauding breathlessly. It was all so clear. How I was going to get there? That part was a little hazy. Especially now, with the baby, I had to admit that my priorities had shifted dramatically. More than anything, I wanted to build a life that Kingston could feel safe and secure in, that would help him grow the wings that would take him to his own freedom. My priorities were nothing like what they'd been even six months ago.

So when Cory said he wanted to manifest a house, I took that seriously. Manifesting a house in Southern California is no small feat, by the way. In the area where we lived, starter homes started at about a half million dollars. If you wanted reliable heat in all of your rooms and maybe a little granite in your kitchen, well, the price went up from there. Of course, that was before the real estate bubble burst and everything began to free-fall. Deep into the Great Recession, you could probably get a starter house on our street for about $400,000, maybe a little less. But that wasn't a safe price because nobody knew how far prices were still going to fall. It was an extremely tricky time. People everywhere were going through tremendous upheaval.

At the same time, the victory is won by those who know what they want and go for it.

"Tell me about the house you want," I said.

"Well, the house needs to have at least four or five bedrooms. And I want the floors in the bathroom to be heated so that when I go to take my shower in the morning my toes don't get cold."

I laughed—hard. "What self-respecting house wouldn't have floor warmers?"

"Right?" he said.

Before I go any further, I must qualify this by saying that my husband was born into an entertainment family in Los Angeles. So to his mind all the things he was mentioning were completely reasonable, nay, necessary for truly civilized living. Somebody had to have a life full of amenities, so why not us? Unfortunately we were in a two-bedroom bungalow on the wrong side of the avenue. Our guesthouse didn't even have central air. Things were pretty touch and go.

Cory and I may have been living in the hills, but we were at the base of the hill. Cory was scheming to move us to the top. In real estate terms, it's a long trek from the bottom to the top of the hill in Los Angeles. A multimillion-dollar trek. But you have to have vision and a long-term goal, right?

Cory was definitely having fun with his vision. Even the baby was getting into it. Every time Cory would list one or another amenity that we simply had to have, the baby would put the exclamation point on it with a loud squeal. It was so much fun I started getting into it too.

"Well, if we're going to do all of that, we'll have to pay for it somehow. So, I think my next book deal needs to be a six-figure deal. At least $350,000."

"Why stop there? Your foreign rights will be worth a lot of money. And the film rights have to be sold. That's at least another $300,000 or $400,000."

"Of course," I agreed. "Not a penny less."

"We should write these things down."

Cory got up and grabbed us both a piece of paper. All jokes aside, we sat down, with the baby between us, and started to write out some things that we wanted to see come into our lives. What did freedom look like for us? How were we going to start shaping the rest of our lives? For me, the most important part of my life, by far, was protecting and providing for our son. He looked to us for absolutely everything. But he also seemed to be coming into an understanding of what he could give, as well as what he needed to receive from us. For example, thus far I'd always been the one doing everything and anything to make him smile. Now he was starting to reciprocate. He would make faces at me to see if I would laugh or smile in return. It was my first indication that he was becoming aware that he could influence his surroundings for the better.

> What did freedom look like? What did creativity and joy look like in our day-to-day lives?

I was taken aback by these daily indicators of how his mind and heart were growing. The need to encourage that growth was so overpowering at times that it took my breath away. So I had to ask the same questions of myself that I wondered about so frequently for him. What did freedom look like? What did creativity and joy look like in our day-to-day lives? It was time to stop being so caught up in the details of our daily tasks that we totally lost sight of the bigger picture. We did need to start naming those possibilities and calling them forth.

We started writing.

Cory scribbled furiously on his side of the dining table. He had a whopper of a list. I, on the other hand, was having a bit more trouble with my list. Finally, I narrowed it down to six things:

- ✓ New house
- ✓ Six-figure book deal
- ✓ Lose 15 pounds (still)
- ✓ Gain insight into the nature of my purpose on the planet
- ✓ Have an audience with the Dalai Lama
- ✓ Be debt-free. No more student loans for me!

I chewed on the edge of my pen, considering. When I took the pen out of my mouth, the baby swiped it, trying to get it into his mouth so he could chew on it too.

"No pen," I said absently. "No pens for babies. Not today. Maybe tomorrow." What did I really want? What was meaningful to me?

Number seven. I thought long and hard about this one. Then I wrote:

- ✓ Have a profound and deeply personal realization of the nature of God in, and as, my life. To embody this truth at a visceral level, releasing all theory about what God is supposed to be, and opening my heart so that I might begin to understand something about what the nature of God truly is.

See. That was all.

And, of course, at the end of my list, I wrote, "This or something better."

"Are you finished now?" Cory asked.

"Um, almost." I was procrastinating. "Let me just look at it one more time."

At the last minute, before we shared our lists, I tacked on at the very bottom of my page in little letters:

✓ I want to travel someplace fun and get my mojo working again.

I almost didn't write that part down, but then I figured, why not?

Cory's list had a lot to do with booking more roles in

> Developing a mind-set of freedom is a completely internal job.

TV shows and commercials, in addition to the multimillion-dollar home. When we exchanged lists, we found ourselves laughing about a lot of it. Most of it. But beneath the laughter was the unspoken understanding that these things represented something much deeper and more fundamental: freedom. They represented the ability to create without restriction.

Developing a mind-set of freedom is a completely internal job. We were both aware that. And, at the same time, sometimes you need to jump-start yourself. We needed to change our way of thinking in order to see our circumstances, and outcomes, in a new light. As the old saying goes, if you do what you've always done, you get what you always got. We both wanted to get some new energy moving through our lives.

By the time the class was set to start, even I was excited. The baby nursed happily—and quietly, thank God—as Kathryn Alice gave the opening remarks. There were a hundred people on the call, all wanting to manifest homes, cars, jobs, husbands, wives, babies, or careers. We began by setting intentions, knowing and declaring exactly what we wanted. Then we learned about the art of allowing these things to unfold in our lives without offering the unconscious resistance that so often denies the very things we desire.

Hmmm.... Boldly declaring exactly what you wanted. That sounded like Kingston to me. Allowing what you want to show up without resistance. Kingston again.

I smiled, thinking that my baby was a master manifester, adept at creating the ideal conditions under which he wanted to live. I looked at him lying in my arms—snug, dry, fat, happy—nursing contentedly without a care in the world. Everything that he needed was provided for him without a moment of worry or thought on his part as to how it would show up. From his perspective, he simply needed something and it appeared. What's more, he fully expected the appearance of every good thing that allowed him to exist in a world in safety and love.

Could it be true that we all had that same power within us to consciously create that which we most desired or needed to experience for our growth and development? Where, I wondered, had that ability gone? If I'd had it, what happened to it?

In short, nothing.

Creativity was an inherent aspect of my being. I was constantly creating, I realized. Every star, every grain of sand, and every cell of our bodies, exists within the same field of constant creation. Each individual life appears for a season, then moves on to create a new path for something else to appear. Even as leaves fall from a tree, more will unfurl from the same branch to take its place. And when the tree dies, some other life is nurtured in its death, whether it's an animal that finds a home in the hollowed-out log, or new shoots sprouting up in the sudden shafts of sunlight that can now spread across the forest floor. There is creativity everywhere. If I was part of that constant creation, if I was a generator of reality, rather than merely a consumer of other people's thoughts *about* reality, that required me to take responsibility for what I was creating.

I finally got the meaning behind the saying *I am 100 percent responsible for my reality.* I'd never quite believed that before. Maybe 85 percent or even 90 percent, but totally responsible? Too many other people had done too many things wrong for me to feel comfortable owning that one. But it was true, nonetheless.

Certainly, I wasn't responsible for what others did. But life required that I take responsibility for my response to what happened in my world, as well as what I allowed others to do in my presence. Whether I chose to embrace a growth mind-set, taking challenges as opportunities to go deeper, or allowed myself to be stunted, the bottom line was that it was all my choice.

I had the choice of creating more of what I wanted in my experience, and less of what I didn't want. Kingston did it every day. He molded the world around him. It astounded me that this tiny boy nursing at my breast, who wasn't even mobile yet, who couldn't crawl, walk, or run, who couldn't hold a conversation or a job, was shaping every aspect of his life in the ways that best suited his growth and development. He was completely dependent, but he was still, in essence, freer than either Cory or myself. It was amazing. It was all about consciousness.

For so long, I'd been creating largely from an unconscious space. My creations were an amalgam of thoughts, fears, worries, and desires, all jumbled up and set loose on the blowing wind. Could I create more accurately? Could I create like Kingston, with tremendous focus and economy, and achieve the results that I really wanted to achieve? This had absolutely nothing to do with the houses and cars and clothing that we had been joking about. No, this was about was purpose, freedom, and creativity. Mastery, I guess.

Conscious creation requires a high degree of self-mastery and awareness along with nonjudgment and compassion. Those are the qualities that I was really looking to experience in my life. I told myself, as I watched the baby drift off to sleep so peacefully, that if I did nothing else, I would open my life to embodying those qualities. That intention might manifest as anything: a novel or another baby or more meditation or more travel. It might look like a willingness to step out of my comfort zone and into uncertainty (because, Lord knows, a comfort zone isn't always comfortable; all that phrase really means is that you're yoked to something familiar, whether you actually like it or not). Whatever it looked like, I was willing to answer to that deeper call.

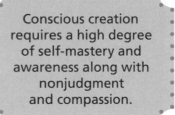

Conscious creation requires a high degree of self-mastery and awareness along with nonjudgment and compassion.

Awakening Bliss: Welcoming Flashes of Unexpected Ecstasy

You can't survive without enchantment.

—THOMAS MOORE

SO MUCH FOR MANIFESTING THE GOOD LIFE.

Our class was still ongoing, but it appeared that the more I concentrated on opening up to the universe and manifesting wisdom and an abundance of good fortune, the more drama rained down on my little head. Everything started falling apart. Apparently I'd brought my winter with me deep into February, rather than shaking off the chill in preparation for spring.

Most of my bad attitude revolved around money worries, something I was admittedly terrible at handling. When things got difficult, I hunched down and wrapped myself up, arming myself against the chill that I imagined pushing at me from every direction. Not exactly the thing to do when you want to manifest good health and abundance. In fact, that's the exact opposite of what you're supposed to do. But knowing this wasn't enough to help me stop doing it. Worse yet, I judged myself for judging my "shortfall."

The Buddhist monk Pema Chödrön wrote: "We can make friends with what we reject, what we see as 'bad' in ourselves and other people. At the same time, we could learn to be generous with what we cherish, what we see as 'good.' If we begin to live in this way, something in us that may have been buried for a long time begins to ripen. Traditionally this 'something' is called bodhicitta, or awakened heart. Something that we already have but usually have not yet discovered. It's as if we were poor, homeless, hungry, and cold, and although we didn't know it, right in the ground where we always slept was a pot of gold."

Had I been somewhat more open (OK, a lot more open), I might have realized that the space I was standing in was a space of answered prayer. I was actually manifesting exactly what I had asked for. Unfortunately, because of the shape that the answers came in, I didn't recognize it at all. It simply felt like a good, old-fashioned hurricane trying to blow me off my feet.

Cory and I looked down at a stack of bills lying in front of us on the dining table, and then looked up at each other. He picked one up.

"Uh, let's get back to this one," Cory said. "Let's look at this one instead."

Cory picked up a bill from Nissan, asking for $1,000 for the last two months' payment on his Z28. Unfortunately, we didn't even have the car. We'd sold it to a friend of mine who owned a car dealership in Virginia. We'd traded in the car to my friend Francis, who'd promised to pay off our note so that he could then sell the car at his dealership. I'd known Francis for more than fifteen years, so we hadn't thought twice about giving him the car, assuming that the check was already in the mail as promised. We turned the car over to his shipping people and waved good-bye with smiles on our faces. The smiles faded pretty quickly when the check never showed up.

We'd expected to have the whole thing cleared up within a few months. More than a year and three months later, we were making payments on the car every month, regardless of the fact that it was sitting in a lot somewhere on the other side of the country. In addition, we were still making our regular payments on the car that we had brought from Francis as part of our "trade in" deal. Thank God we were able to do it. But with me not working regularly over the past few months, well, things were finally starting to catch up with us.

I bristled inside. I didn't want to pay the bill, even though none of this was Nissan's fault at all. More than the money, I was angry about the idea that someone I'd known and trusted for so many years could callously disregard his word and our well-being. He walked away, seemingly without a backward glance. That was hard—almost as hard as it was to file the paperwork to sue him for breach of contract and auto theft. But the worst part was finding out that we were at the end of a very long list of people who were attempting to sue my old buddy Francis. On top of all that, the FBI was after him too. The bottom line was that we weren't getting our money back. At least not without divine intervention. We'd be lucky if we got the car back, which we'd recently found out that he had also crashed.

Was this abundance? Some nights, after Kingston and

Cory were asleep, I'd lie awake asking if this was where I was supposed to start seeing the goodness that moved in mysterious ways, beyond circumstances? Maybe my vision was still too cloudy. At this point, unshakable faith was supposed to kick in along with the knowing that we were provided for in miraculous ways. Right? It sounded good. I believe it completely.

In theory.

Actually, I had a few reservations. Well, more than a few. I feared it was all a load of bunk, truth be told, a lot of airy-fairy, spiritual mumbo jumbo. In my heart, I wanted nothing more than to hold fast to my beliefs and to see that faith outpictured as peace and serenity, as well as new ideas and concrete, actionable steps. But when the rubber met the road, I found myself coming up short in the faith department. Day after day, the mail lady would push the mail (read: bills) through the mail slot, where the letters slipped helplessly to the floor. And I would leave them there, making a bigger and bigger pile each day. In my mind, the letters looked like kindling waiting for a match. It was hard to fall back on what I knew, particularly with such a relentless mail lady who continued to march so audaciously up our front steps every afternoon. Shame on her.

But isn't that what growth is all about? Practicing what you know even in the most difficult moments. I knew that too. Unfortunately, it didn't make it any easier to actually do what I knew.

"Hello? Hello?" Cory said. "Are you still there? You look like you checked out."

"I'm still here," I mumbled. "What were we talking about?"

"We were talking about the insurance payment on the Z. They still want $250 a month for the car. I've contacted them and told them we don't have the car anymore, but they still sent the bill."

Surprise, surprise.

"Hello?"

"What?"

"I said, what do you think we should do?"

I was absolutely no help. I couldn't process any of it anymore. I wanted to crawl into bed and snuggle with the baby and pull the covers up over my head and sleep until spring. Let the winter be over when we woke up.

I don't do well when money is low. Poverty creeps me out. I get claustrophobic and panicky. Nobody likes being broke, but I have a physical aversion to scarcity. Perhaps it comes from growing up poor. There were times when I lived for days on popcorn and biscuits that I made myself out of flour, water, and lard. Clearly, starvation would have been the healthier option. But what did I know?

We lived way out by the Whitestone Bridge in the Bronx. By the time I was thirteen, I was getting up at five in the morning and walking over two miles to the subway in the dark to take the train downtown to Lincoln Center to get to school.

I had initiated all of this myself, and did it quite gladly, so that I could go to a good school—not the zoned school in my neighborhood, where dead bodies had been found in the abandoned field outside the main building.

I knew what poverty looked like, and it was ugly. I didn't want anything to do with it. I had always prided myself on paying all bills in full on time and going where I wanted to go and doing what I wanted to do. Period. Feeling frozen by my fear didn't just affect my ability to move forward in decisive ways, but even my ability to think fluidly. My mind was too slushy to be able to read and understand what those people were asking for. To be facing such pressure with a little baby to take care of, well, the import of that wasn't lost on me.

This was the time of my life when I felt the most vulnerable, the most in need of space and stability. I knew there had to be a great breakthrough waiting on the other end of this. There had to be. The universe would have to be pretty screwed up if there wasn't. Cory, God bless his heart, always tried to put a positive spin on everything. As he sorted the bills into actionable piles, he continued to try to reassure me.

"Don't worry," he said. "I'm sure we can work all this out. I'll call all these guys in the morning. Don't worry. Maybe I can even get some of these payments lowered. Either way you look at it, we are still abundant, right? We're still manifesting things!"

He smiled and I couldn't help but smile back. Actually, my smile looked more like a grimace, like I'd just stubbed my toe or something. I couldn't quite make it all the way to happy. But I did try for a second.

"Oh, I think I hear the baby. I'll be right back."

I headed toward the back room, even though I knew Kingston was fast asleep. I just needed a moment alone. My body started itching for a big gulp of Pepsi and a mound of chocolate cake. Self-medicating with sugar is perhaps my worst vice. Obviously, Pepsi and cake wasn't the meal of champions for a nursing mother. But still, I found myself wondering how fast I could make it to the convenience store and back. I tiptoed into the bedroom, thinking there had to be more constructive ways to deal with stress. Maybe I could take a bubble bath or meditate or...

What else? I couldn't think of anything for a good, long minute.

Aha! Maybe I could pray my way out of this mess. Or I could tithe my way out. But that felt too much like trying to bribe God. Something about that just didn't sound right. I had the strange feeling that it probably wouldn't work, anyway.

I got undressed for bed, thinking, *You could always go look for a nine-to-five job.* The thought of it made my heart sink. Leaving my son for nine or ten or eleven hours a day when he was so small and still needed me so much didn't feel right. I wasn't ready for that yet. I'd been a freelancer most of my adult life. I'd always been able to make up money when I needed it. Why not now? There had to be another way to address the situation we were in. Life was asking us to step into a space where peace of mind could operate freely, regardless of circumstance. Peace and acceptance had the power to create a wide-open doorway for abundance and joy.

I could see what joy looked like. It was lying there in the bedroom, blissfully curled up on its side, with a little arm flung over its face, snoring softly. It was wearing blue and brown *I'm Not Sleepy Yet* pajamas. That was bliss. I felt bliss when I stopped long enough to look him in the face and truly take him in. When I was aware of bliss, I was aware of all the possibilities that it represented, and all the possibility that was within me, waiting for permission to be activated. It was all there at my fingertips. But I needed to be able to access it consciously and consistently.

It wasn't enough to believe that abundance and confidence and power are the natural state of my being. I wanted to tease out the manifestation of these qualities into my daily living, bringing them from just beyond my fingertips to right within my grasp. I went to sleep with those thoughts lying motionless on the pillow beside my head.

The next morning, I woke up to Kingston cooing right next to me, laughing about something that I could only guess at. He rolled from his

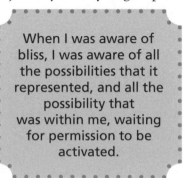

When I was aware of bliss, I was aware of all the possibilities that it represented, and all the possibility that was within me, waiting for permission to be activated.

back onto his belly until he was nose to nose with me as I opened my eyes.

"Good morning, sweet love, how are you?"

He smiled at me, then opened up his wide mouth and chomped down on my nose.

"Thank you, my love. Mommy needed a little bit of spit to start the morning off just right. Okay, let's get up and change that diapy."

The wonderful thing about co-sleeping, I have to honestly say, is that I hadn't had a bad morning in six months. There was no greater joy than waking up to a wide-eyed, smiling baby. Now, what happened after I got out of bed could be hit or miss, depending on the day. But in order to experience true contentment, all I had to do was open my eyes in the morning.

I scooped the baby up. He was so warm and delicious, just flushed with well-being. But even when he was grumpy, even when storm clouds crossed his little face, he was still just as yummy. One of the most glorious things about Kingston was that no matter what was going on inside his little world, he stayed so gloriously perfect at his core—at least in my eyes. It didn't matter whether he was screaming and fussing or sleeping peacefully in my arms. I was able to see the truth of who he was, and who I was in relation to him. It's a gift of mommies everywhere: to see the light of God made flesh in an infant's face. And the sight is awesome.

There was no circumstance or situation that could change

that knowing for me. That was what being unmovable looked like and felt like. What would happen, I wondered, if I could transfer that understanding from this one area of my life to the other areas where, apparently, circumstance was kicking my butt?

Cory was already gone that morning. He'd gotten up early for an audition and had gone straight to work at Agape from there. So baby and I dressed for our day pretty leisurely. I carried him into the bathroom so I could take my shower. We had a beautiful bathroom with black marble walls and floors. It had a huge whirlpool tub and glass shower with a seafoam-green vessel sink next to it, and an oversized vanity mirror over the sink. Just opposite were floor-to-ceiling mirrors that lined the wall of the walk-in closet. Yes, the bathroom was my favorite room in the house. I put Kingston into his giraffe bouncy seat and let him play in front of the closet mirror while I showered.

I was feeling so good that I almost walked up the steps and turned the faucet on the whirlpool tub, instead of taking a shower. But that would've taken too long. Baby would not have stood for that. He had a good fifteen minutes in a bouncy seat before he'd be letting me know that I needed to get a move on. So I opted for the quick shower while he happily entertained himself in front of the mirror, making faces at his reflection. I watched him play through the glass doors of the shower. Every so often, the doors would steam up a little bit and I would quickly rub the steam away to make sure that I could still see his face. It occurred to me that I was really, super spoiled. I loved my life. I wanted it to stay exactly the way it was. Just better.

But even as I was still thinking the thought, the voice inside my head said, Accept change. It will always be for the better, no matter how it may look in the moment.

I didn't know quite what to make of that. Change? What kind of change? I wanted change as in more money and more time to myself every once in a while. I liked that kind of change. I didn't want other kinds of change, the could-be-seen-as-part-of-a-downward-spiral kinds of change. Once again I liked my life too much. I liked my bathroom too much. I liked our overly warm guesthouse and our neighborhood and our neighbors next door, Donna, who was a judge, and Cecilia, who was a professor. The neighbors on the other side of us had rowdy teenagers who liked to blast horrible music in the middle of the afternoon and park their car on the lawn rather than in the driveway like people with sense. I could've done without them. But they came with the package and I was willing to accept that, lest the universe think I was being nitpicky and ungrateful.

I loved having parties and people over. It dawned on me that part of the anxiety and agitation that had been following me around for weeks had to do with the feeling (the fear) that things were about to change drastically. I didn't want drastic change. I wanted a little bit of change here and there, in the places that needed tweaking. I wanted the things that

I believed would make me happier, a little freer.

Clearly, somewhere in that thought process there was a small bit of contradiction going on.

Unfortunately, I didn't have the energy to sit and contemplate where that contradiction might be hiding, try to root it out and get myself into real, authentic alignment. Instead, I stepped out of the shower, brushed my teeth, and got dressed. Then I scooped up Kingston and got him dressed. It seemed like it might be a good idea to take a nice long walk. Maybe I'd come up with some new ideas for another creative writing class to make some extra money to keep things on an even keel. That seemed like a responsible, concrete plan of action.

So we left the house and walked up the hill, looking at all the beautiful bungalows that we passed along the way, some of them with ornate gardens out front and beautiful palm trees and pines. Birds

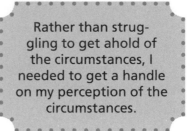

Rather than struggling to get ahold of the circumstances, I needed to get a handle on my perception of the circumstances.

flew overhead, darting in circles around us. Just as we got to the corner, two iridescent hummingbirds swooped down from the palm tree to our left, stopping almost directly in front of our faces. Kingston was facing forward in his baby carrier. He squealed in delight as they circled around and took off again into the sky. He flapped his little arms like he was trying to fly away too. The wonder of it all was undeniable. There was so much that was right with life, so much good going on at every moment. It was up to me to choose where to place my attention. Rather than struggling to get ahold of the circumstances, I needed to get a handle on my perception of the circumstances.

We continued to walk, taking in everything that we encountered: the traffic, the trees, the barking dogs, the white kittens that roamed our street, making the entire neighborhood their playground. They darted in and out of people's rosebushes and across their driveways. These were the same cats that loved to antagonize our Miko. They regularly came to pee on our garden wall for the sole purpose of upsetting my pretty girl by marking her territory as their own. These were the same cats that I threw shoes at when they came skulking into my backyard. But they were picture-perfect adorable when they were in front of somebody else's house. Again, go figure.

It took us almost an hour to reach Agape. When we did, I felt clear and refreshed. The walk had done its job. We headed up to the main building. As we walked into the parking lot, I saw Rev. Michael walking out to his car.

"Hey," he called over to us. "How you be?"

"Oh, you know, I be all right."

"What do you mean all right? What's going on, little man," he said, shaking his dreadlocks in the baby's face. Kingston laughed and grabbed at them. He wasn't fast enough, but he was ready to try again.

"Be careful," I said. "You might not get one of those back."

Michael wiggled his locks again, tickling the baby's nose. "So, what's going on with you?"

I shrugged. "I'm just going through some things."

"Yeah? Tell me about it."

"I don't know. There's just a lot of stuff, a lot of crap. It's kind of hard for me to put my finger on it."

"Could you be a little more specific?"

"Things are…a lot different than I thought they would be."

"I see. You had some expectations about what life was supposed to look like at this point and those expectations have set you up for disappointment. Uh-huh. Go on."

"Well, if you already know the story—"

"Go on."

I wasn't sure how to say what I wanted to say without devolving into a complaint.

> If you want to wake up you walk directly into the storm.

"There's just a lot of change happening right now. I feel like it's getting the best of me and I don't know how to stop that."

"I hear you," he said. "Life doesn't work out the way we think we want it to a lot of the time. But remember, you have the choice to stop looking at what's wrong and start looking toward what is right and what you want to experience."

"That's funny. I just thought about that a little while ago. But don't I have to at least acknowledge what's wrong to try to make it right?"

He laughed. "That's not how you make it right, though.

You got it backward. You look at what's right first, because that's the truth."

"What if the truth is that I'm worrying way too much about money and responsibility and—"

"The truth is that you are abundance. That's the real truth, above and beyond anything that may be happening right now. You are abundance itself. When you get frustrated by circumstances or caught up in fear, doubt, and worry, your awareness of truth is the first thing that vanishes. Unless you develop a practice for seeing rightly."

"I just want to feel like I'm getting back into control of my life. You know what I mean?"

"Of course. You're growing and maturing and part of that process is understanding that we don't have to know every answer to every question that life throws at us. We don't have to tame the seas. We just have to sail them. When we're young, it's very natural to feel like everything has to be going the way you want in order to feel safe and secure. But that's not where real safety comes from. That's not where security and joy come from. That's not where you wake up. In fact, it's the exact opposite. If you want to wake up you walk directly into the storm."

"Okay, you're going to have to say that again."

He smiled, my godfather guru. "The goal is to stand in the middle of the storm because that's where the gift is. Whatever you're facing, that situation or circumstance is calling you to a higher level of being. You find the strength and fortitude to activate that awareness by standing within the midst of the storm and becoming one with it. Then you know that it can't hurt you. It can only grow you."

"Well, I'm being grown a whole lot," I said.

He laughed. "That's true. This is an incredible growth period, for both of you. It's beautiful to watch. You'll move through it and eventually stop allowing the circumstance to dictate whether you live your life in joy, peace, and love. Then you get to the point where there's nothing that can take your happiness. There's nothing that can take your sense of peace and oneness. It simply becomes who you are. It has absolutely nothing to do with any circumstance that may come your way. It is what is. And it's usually not the good things in life that get us to that point of embodiment. It's usually the gifts of the storm that help mold us into that space. If we stop resisting, we become more open to receive whatever gift the storm has come to give. It's a choice."

"What if I make the wrong choice?"

"You can't make the wrong choice. No matter what you choose, you're going to continue to grow and learn just like he does," he said, nodding to the baby. "But if you can train yourself to stand in your peace in the same way that the baby embodies his bliss, you'll get to live the fruits of that choice. Does that make sense? You don't want to stand still. You don't want the storm to stop. You don't want to just coast, because then you don't grow."

Sometimes it's so hard for me to give an inch. "I don't

know if I want to grow that much, that fast."

"But then," he said, "would you want to live with yourself for the rest of your life exactly the way you are right now?"

I thought about that, with my up-and-down and up-and-down and sideways emotions, not being able to count on my own moods from one moment to the next, and very quickly said, "Oh, no. I really don't need to be with that for eternity."

"Then you're moving in the right direction," Rev. Michael said. "You're exactly where you need to be."

"I'll take your word for it," I said.

"And that's good enough for right now," he replied, smiling.

My Six-Month-Old Is Faster Than I Am: Taking Chances

Security is mostly a superstition. It does not exist in nature, nor do the children of men as a whole experience it. Avoiding danger is no safer in the long run than outright exposure. Life is either a daring adventure or nothing.

—HELEN KELLER

KINGSTON ROLLED FROM HIS BACK ONTO HIS TUMMY AND wiggled his butt. He threw an arm out over his head and grabbed his blanket, trying to army-crawl away from me while giggling like a little madman.

"Oh, no, you don't, Mr. Baby," I said. "You are not going anywhere."

He growled in protest as I picked him up off the floor and carried him to the changing table.

"Just where do you think you're going, anyway? Are you trying to make for the border? That's two hours away from here, man. You need your license before you can drive the 405."

He giggled, pulling at my hair. I laid him down on the table, making sure to keep one hand on his tummy as I reached down to get a diaper. Kingston grabbed my hand, pulled it up to his mouth, and bit me. Hard.

"Owww! Cut that out," I said. "That actually hurt."

He completely ignored me, gnawing contentedly on my flesh. Kingston was now six months old and his first two teeth had poked through a couple of weeks before. My little baby was becoming such a big boy. Now he was at the stage of chewing anything he could get his hands on.

"Mr. Baby, you are not allowed to eat the mommy. If you eat off my hand I won't be able to change your diaper. How can I keep my hand on your tummy if I don't have one?"

The baby screamed, happy to ignore me some more.

"Come back here, little mischief baby," I said as he tried to roll away again. I fastened the diaper and scooped him up, carrying him over to the bed where I had his little outfit laid out. I pulled on his shirt, a pair of jeans, and some clean sneaker socks to match the shirt.

"There," I said. "Now you're presentable for Nana and Aaron and Avery. Everyone is coming to see you tonight. Isn't that great?"

Kingston couldn't have cared less. He was too busy chewing on my hair now.

"No hair for you. Not today."

He dropped his head down a bit, mouthing on my neck and shoulders.

"Kingston, would you stop eating me? I am not a tasty treat. I am not candy. I am not cake. Will you please leave Mommy alone?"

"What's that little man up to?" Cory asked as we walked out into the living room.

"He's eating me again."

"You come here. You want to chew on somebody? You chew on me. I'm much tougher than Mama, but that just means you can chew on me for longer."

Cory kissed the baby's cheek and took him to sit on the

sofa in the living room. We had a few minutes before Cory's mom and his niece and nephew arrived for dinner. I was hoping that his brother Tari and our sister-in-law Aquita would be coming also, but no luck there. For whatever reason, they had decided to stay home. I'd also called one of my other best friends, Lisa, and her husband, Glenn, to see if they wanted to come. No dice there either. It was just us, Nana, and kids.

My mother-in-law, Elaine, was bringing dinner for us, which was sweet of her. She did that periodically, as in, "You guys must be hungry! You shouldn't have to cook again. Don't worry, I'll cook dinner and while you eat I can play with the baby!"

She and the kids loved being with Kingston. Avery was ten years old and smart as she could be. Aaron was almost eight and quite the handful of littleboyness. Whenever I managed to land a kiss on his cheek you would've thought that the toxins from my girl-spit were going to melt him into a puddle of slime on the ground. But he was cute as a button and he adored the baby. I could tell because no matter how much Kingston slobbered on him, he never complained. And if there was one thing Aaron could do, it was complain. He was very discriminating in his preferences.

The doorbell rang. Cory and Kingston jumped up to answer it. I could hear the commotion as they ushered everyone in from the chilly night air.

"Well, hello, Kuwana," Elaine said, her eyes fastened on the baby. "How are you?"

"I'm doing well, thank you," I said.

"Hi, Auntie Kuwana." Avery hugged me tight around the waist and I kissed her forehead.

"Hello, Aaron," I called.

"Hey," he mumbled and flung himself down on the couch.

"Let me see this little bubba boo," Elaine sang.

Kingston clapped his hands for his Nana and waved his little feet in the air. He had been saying the word *nana* since he was two months old, much to her delight. I knew it was just mimicry, but still, if he had such sharp ears why hadn't he said the word *mama* yet? Everyone settled in around the baby and started making small talk. But really, we were all still embarrassingly fascinated, just waiting to see what he would do next. True to form, Kingston played the room. He was a born performer, batting his eyelashes and making silly faces.

"I hope you all are hungry," Elaine said. "I brought Mexican lasagna with salad and cornmeal-crusted, pan-fried tilapia with a chipotle sauce on the side. Oh, yes, and there's a pear tart for dessert."

One nice thing about having my mother-in-law come over was that we could always eat for a week after her visits. We sat down to the table while Cory dished up everyone's food. Kingston's eyes widened as he stared at all the food piling up in front of us. It smelled ridiculously good, so good in fact that I felt bad that he wasn't able to eat any. Apparently, so did he. He practically flung himself into my plate.

"Hold on, Baby," I said. "This food is not for you."

Kingston disagreed. Anytime I brought a forkful of food toward my mouth, he tried to grab the handle and redirect it to him. Finally, I took a small bowl down from the kitchen shelf and dished up a little bit of the lasagna, some tortilla, beans, and chipotle sauce. Then I mushed it up really good. Out of curiosity more than anything else, I fed Kingston a spoonful to see what he would do.

The moment that food touched his mouth he screamed with such delight that everyone at the table fell out laughing. Mexican lasagna was definitely a hit. He finished off the bowl within minutes and demanded seconds. It made sense. Kingston wasn't the type of baby who would go for puréed anything. I'd tried to give him various cereals and baby food, only to have him spit it out with a scowl. Kingston was spicy, so why not his food? He was always ready to do something different. His excitement was palpable and contagious.

"I knew it!" Elaine crowed. "This baby is a foodie. He's got such a discriminating palate."

Kingston had just gotten on his Nana's good side for life. He ate himself into a stupor and was already half asleep by the time dinner was over. He didn't even know it when Elaine and the kids quietly headed out on the long drive back to the Valley.

I tucked him into bed in just his diaper. He lay open-mouthed and snoring like a little drunken man, with his hand draped over his stuffed belly. Cory and I watched him, trying not to laugh and wake him up again. Kingston was so contented, so satisfied. I felt full just looking at him.

He was changing right before my eyes in ways that, weeks ago, I would never have been able to fathom. Every day something new occurred to him. Every day he was able to do more, quicker, faster, easier. He had always been a social animal. Even as a newborn, he would hold the eyes of people who spoke to him, as though he fully understood what they were saying, though he didn't quite have the capability to respond.

Well, now he was responding, albeit in his baby language. It fascinated me when we had conversations, me asking questions or making remarks and observations, while he responded confidently with squeals and grunts. I made up what I thought his answers meant and he never seemed to mind, so long as I continued with the conversations. And he wanted to talk about everything. Sometimes he even talked in his sleep, going over the events of the day, cataloging and commenting. It really was just like my friend Lisa had once told me: How they are inside the belly is exactly how they are when they come out of the belly. Kingston had given us fair warning. He was nothing if not consistent.

The next day, I decided to put our leftovers to good use and asked Lisa to come over on her lunch break. Lisa and I had known each other for years. She was from Northern California and had moved to Los Angeles to further her law career. But with a husband and two children, she'd made the choice to put the law degree away for a while because of the long hours and demands. Instead, she opted to take a position as the director of learning resources at one of the top private schools in Southern California, where her children attended. Her husband also worked at a nearby private school, so all four of them basically had the same work hours during the week, and the same holiday schedule. They'd made big sacrifices in order to have the time and energy to devote to their family, but ultimately it seemed to work for everyone. Lisa's family seemed to be one of the happiest that I knew.

As soon as I saw her pulling up out front I opened the door wide, waving.

"Hi there!" she said. "Oh my goodness, what is cooking in this house?"

"Nana came to visit last night."

"Ooohhh. Can Nana come to my house too? Oh, my God. Look at this big boy. He is so gorgeous. How do you stand it?"

Kingston smiled, pleased with the complement.

She held the baby close and danced a little step with him. "I know I say it every time, but I can't believe how big he's getting. It's amazing. I remember when he was in the belly and we were driving back from Las Vegas. You were so big I thought for sure that you were gonna have that baby in the desert."

I laughed. "By that time I was ready to have the baby in the desert. I just wanted him to come!"

"I remember when I was pregnant with Michelle, I couldn't

think of anything more wonderful than to be able to see my feet again. How's it going for you guys?"

"He's running me ragged. I can't keep up with him. He's changing so fast. Every day it's something new. It's exciting, but kind of scary," I admitted.

"Oh, embrace it. Change is great. Before you know it, he'll be crawling and walking and running and wanting to do everything for himself. Enjoy it. You mark my words—it only gets better from here."

This was the second time I'd heard basically the same advice in the space of two days. There was a shift going on in Kingston's world. These changes were opportunities for his growth, as well as my own. What other reason could there be for me to hear the same words again? All through lunch, I wondered quietly when I had become so adverse to change. When had I become such a fuddy-duddy? I used to be the queen of newness. The adventurer, remember? When had that shifted? I didn't know, but I wanted to shift it back.

Lisa only had about a half an hour before she had to turn around and drive back to school. Lunch seemed to be over before it started. But it was just as well. I didn't even get the door closed all the way before Kingston started giving me the milk face. His lunch had worn off already. Well, he was a growing, changing boy.

As he nursed, I gave myself a little pep talk: *I embrace change. It's nothing to be nervous about.* In fact, to show life what a good sport I was, I set an intention. I resolved to take

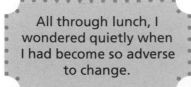

All through lunch, I wondered quietly when I had become so adverse to change.

the very next opportunity that came my way to do something new. It didn't matter what it was—I would say yes and let change happen.

As I was busy congratulating myself and feeling pretty good, I noticed the time. We had a bunch of errands to run for the afternoon and time was wasting. I couldn't leave the house without checking my e-mail quickly, so I set Kingston down for a moment and logged on to my account. A friend had referred a new writing client to me and I wanted to see whether the person had responded to my e-mail.

I opened up my inbox and the first thing I noticed was a message from another girlfriend, Tangie. Tangie was a mother of two and a very successful television actress. In a business so full of low self-esteem and cynicism, Tangie was a fountain of joyful positivity. In fact, her trademark greeting was "Heaven high!" because *hello* ("Hell" "low," get it?) had a decidedly unsavory vibration. If you didn't laugh when Tangie was around, you probably didn't have a working sense of humor to start with.

The e-mail was a forward from a game show producer she knew. I almost deleted it on the spot. But, since it had come from Tangie, I figured it was worth twelve seconds of my time. The Game Show Network was holding auditions for *The Newlywed Game*. They wanted couples who had been married less than two years to appear on the show and duke it out for a chance to win an all-expenses-paid second honeymoon to some fabulously exotic location.

Again my index finger hovered over the delete key. Me, on a game show? Me, the serious thinker, the author, the intellect and scholar, on—*The Newlywed Game*? Really, come on. My snooty finger was poised and ready to strike when I remembered the promise I'd made not even five minutes earlier. I was going to say yes to the very next opportunity that came my way. No matter what it was.

But surely the universe didn't mean this, I thought, looking down my nose at the computer. What I'd been envisioning was more along the lines of a new book deal (even though my manuscript was nowhere near complete or submission ready. But details like that were irrelevant where the power of the universe was concerned. Someone, somewhere had the ability to find me, if they really wanted to).

But a magical book deal did not present itself to me. *The Newlywed Game* did. What else could I do? I opened the attachment and filled out the application. Instead of hitting the delete key, I hit send. *There you go, Great God of the Universe. I did it. Now I have fulfilled my end of the bargain.* As far as I was concerned, I was off the hook.

The next morning, when I opened my e-mail, I saw a response from the producer, asking Cory and me to come in for an audition. Now this was getting ridiculous. This little game that the universe was playing was going a bit too far. I wasn't really sure that I wanted to continue to entertain it.

But then I looked over at Kingston, who was on his back on the floor, pedaling his fat legs in the air like he was in the home stretch of the Tour de France, and I thought, *What's the problem? Why not? It's not like you've never been on a game show before. And, remember, last time you won $5,000. Not bad for a day's work.*

Cory was headed out the door just at that moment.

"Hey, babe, do you want to go with me on an audition?" I said.

His ears immediately pricked up. My husband's favorite two words were "an audition."

"An audition for what?"

I'd stopped auditioning long ago, so Cory was intrigued, but a little bit suspicious.

"Oh, you know, just a game show," I said.

He frowned. "A game show? Uh, I don't think so. I'm an actor. I don't do game shows."

Now whose nose was stuck in the air? Just because he said no, I got a little defensive. Maybe I wanted to do *The Newly-wed Game.* I came rushing to my little game show's rescue.

"Why not? It's not like we don't qualify. I just got an e-mail saying they want us to come in for an audition next Monday. How about it?"

Monday was Cory's day off.

"Well, I *guess* I could go. What do you get if you win?"

"I'm not sure yet. But I just thought it might be a fun outing, like a date night. We haven't been anywhere in months."

You know you live in LA when you have to be "camera ready" for your date night.

"Maybe we'll take an hour or two and go see what it's about," I offered nonchalantly. "Maybe your mom can watch the baby. Hey, maybe she can even come to the studio with us, since I'm sure it won't take too long. Then we can all hang out and go to lunch after. What do you think?"

"You know, that could be fun. Tell them yes. Why not?"

I e-mailed the producer and within three hours received a reply telling us all the parameters of the audition process. I skimmed over the long e-mail. *Blah, blah, blah... So on and so forth...* Then I got halfway down the page and saw the line that read, "Be prepared to be on set for a minimum of eight to ten hours."

There went that idea.

Too bad. Just when I was starting to get warmed up to the idea of auditioning again, they had to go and blow it. Oh, well. I called Cory at Agape and told him that it wasn't going to work out.

"Why not?" he asked.

I explained to him that they would need us to be available for at least eight hours.

"Yeah? So?"

Hello? Had he forgotten the little drooling guy that stayed attached to my boob practically every moment of the day?

"We can't leave the baby for that long," I said uncomfortably.

"Well, my mom doesn't work on Mondays, so she would probably be willing to watch the baby all day. As a matter of fact, I'm sure she'd love it."

"Eight hours? Are you kidding? What would happen when he needed a nap or if he needed his diaper changed?"

"My mother can change a diaper like anybody else."

"Well, he gets fussy sometimes," I insisted. "What happens if he gets fussy?"

"Then she'll get him unfussy. What's going on? What's the problem?"

The real problem was answered prayer. Change. In the six months that Kingston had been on the planet, he and I had never been separated from each other for more than an hour or two at a time. Small as it might seem to some people, leaving him all day would be a huge step for me. Just the idea of being away from him for that long made me feel off-center. Of course, in the grand scheme of things it wasn't a very long time. It's not like I was going to be gone a week or two. Many, many parents did it every single day when they went off to work, and the world didn't stop spinning. The babies didn't forget about them while they were gone. The parents came home at dinnertime and all was well.

But somehow being rational didn't help. I was scared.

"I'm going to have to think about it," I said. Then I hung up on Cory really quick before he could say anything logical.

Baby and I went to the park that afternoon. I held him close in his carrier as we walked past the amphitheater in the park off La Brea Avenue. We walked across the stage and then slowly through the low stone seats, almost like we were going through a rite of passage. It kind of was. He had been born into a family of artists. It was something he would have to get used to. Stages were going to be part of his life, in one way or another, forever.

The pines and the eucalyptus trees towered over us. We climbed back onto the stage, which echoed with our footsteps in such a sweet way. I wondered if Kingston felt it too. I'd always wanted to be an actress, but somewhere along the way I lost that vision. I'd changed. And that was one change that I didn't always see as being for the better. Perhaps that was why, and when, I began to feel the need to control things. On a fundamental level, I started to shy away from real challenges, to go the safe way.

But if these were the unspoken realities of my life, then this is what my son would be watching and learning from as I made all my decisions moving forward.

It had to stop.

"You like hanging out with Nana, don't you?" I asked the baby. "Nana's fun. She loves playing and making funny faces at you. You enjoy that sort of thing, right?"

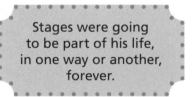

Stages were going to be part of his life, in one way or another, forever.

Kingston put his little hand up to my cheek and patted it.
"All right. We'll do it."

The next Monday, Nana was knocking on our front door at 8:00 a.m., full of smiles.

"I'm getting over a little bit of a cold today. It was kind of hard to get out of the bed, so I'm glad I'm not late."

I sure couldn't tell any of that. She looked bright-eyed and happy to me, like she couldn't get us out the door fast enough. She kissed the baby all over his face and he laughed, excited by her excitement.

"Maybe we'll even watch a little bit of *Sesame Street* today," she sing-songed. "What do you think? Do you like Elmo yet?"

"No!" Cory yelled from the back of the house.

Cory is the only person on planet Earth who hates Elmo. When it comes to Elmo, his happy-go-lucky personality turns ominous.

"Well, it doesn't matter what you think about Elmo, because you are leaving today and Nana is here. All right, Bubby. Wave bye-bye!"

And with that, I was obsolete. No longer necessary. Cory set a milk bottle out where Elaine could find it. Then he put the rest in the refrigerator. That was it.

"By the way," I stalled, "in case you missed it, I made his lunch. It's right here on this shelf in the refrigerator. I also made him a snack, some fresh organic applesauce with a little bit of Vietnamese cinnamon. He likes cinnamon. That's in this container right here, next to the milk. There's even a little bit of rice on the shelf below it—"

"I'm sure I'll be able to find it," Elaine said, eyeing the refrigerator, "in these neatly labeled containers. How...helpful. Now, stop worrying. Just go and have a great time!"

"Oh, and just so you know, the phones might be off. So if you call our cell phones and don't get any answer, just leave a message. Because I'll be checking. I'm going to turn the phone back on to check for your messages. We're not supposed to use our phones while were on the lot, but I don't care what they say. I'm doing it anyway. So if you need anything—"

"Have a good time," she said, smiling, and gave us an extra firm wave.

Cory dragged me out the door to the car. We drove north up La Brea Avenue. As we rode past Kenneth Hahn Park, the Hollywood sign stood out proudly from behind a dissipating layer of smog. It looked shiny and promising in the morning sun, until another smog cloud covered it up again. The sign played peekaboo for the next few minutes, taunting me.

We arrived at the studio on Sunset Boulevard in Hollywood about a half hour later and started our long wait. The producers hadn't been kidding. We were really there all day long. Periodically, they asked us questions about who we were and why we got married. Then they asked us to tell everyone the most interesting thing that happened to us when we first got engaged.

Cory told the story of how we climbed to the top of Mount Kilimanjaro. He had had the diamond ring in his pocket, planning every step of the way how he would get down on one knee at the top of the world, buffeted by the snows of Kiliman-jaro, and ask for my hand in marriage. However, when we got about two hours below the summit, I sat down on a rock and proceeded to throw my guts up from altitude sickness.

"No, that's it for you," our guide, Boniface, said to me. "It's the end of the road. You're going back down. Cory, you can keep going. You're fine."

"No," said Cory, clasping the ring in his pocket. "No, I'll go back down with her."

"Don't be ridiculous," Boniface insisted. "You keep going. We have another porter. He can go up with you the rest of the way."

"*I said* it's all right. I'll go back down."

None of us knew that I had just foiled Cory's elaborately thought out plan.

"Will you just get out of here?" I scolded him. "There's no reason for both of us to miss the summit. What's wrong with you?"

"I. Said. No."

"Why not?"

"Because...my toes are cold," Cory growled.

We were quiet for a beat, like, *Did you just hear that too?* Then we let him have it.

"Oooohhh! Cory's toes are cold!" I taunted. "He's not going to go up the mountain 'cause his toes are too cold! Wait, babe. I thought you brought your toe warmers with you. What happened to them?"

We tormented him for the next 17,000 feet, down through five different climate zones, all the way down to the foot of the mountain. *Poor Cory, poor little California boy. Cold toes? How gut-wrenching! The hardship! The agony!*

I'm surprised he still asked me to marry him after all that. But he did. Eventually. The way Cory told the story was really hilarious. He had everyone in the room howling

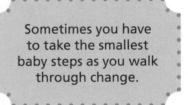

Sometimes you have to take the smallest baby steps as you walk through change.

with laughter. By the end of the day, they had invited us to come back for a taping of the show.

"Oh, no, no, no," I said. "Thanks, but no thanks. That would be another whole day, maybe even longer than this day."

"We'll be there," Cory told them.

I grimaced at Cory. Then I smiled thinly at the PA and said, "Yes, of course. We'll be there."

Sometimes you have to take the smallest baby steps as you walk through change.

Perhaps, I thought, *I could learn a few new things about myself along the way. Or I could relearn some things that I already knew.*

We went back a week later. As it turned out, all the angst was worth it. I won my first manifestation: an all-expenses-paid trip for the three of us to Kauai.

Imagine that.

The Precursor of the Mirror Is the Mother's Face: Trusting Your Power

Leave the mirror and change your face. Leave the world alone and change your conceptions of yourself.

—NEVILLE GODDARD

I SAT AT THE DINING TABLE WITH THE COMPUTER OPEN IN front of me again, staring at the unopened file. The book was like a little devil that kept whispering in my ear and wouldn't go away. Six months before, I would've called it an angel, but times change.

The more I tried to get back into it, the harder it seemed to write anything fresh or interesting.

After staring at the screen awhile longer, I got frustrated and decided to shut it off. Better to come back and try again another time. I looked at the clock on my phone: 2:12 a.m. The baby would be awake again in five hours. I got up, turned off all the lights, and locked the doors before heading to the bedroom.

As quietly as I could, I undressed and climbed into the bed. Kingston was asleep next to Cory. Somehow, even though he was the size of a Build-A-Bear, he managed to take up three-quarters of the bed. I moved him gently, trying to eke out a little bit of space for myself. As though he'd been waiting for me, his eyes popped open and his little head swiveled in my direction. *Oh great*, I thought. Kingston usually didn't wake up at night. When he was hungry, he mewled and whined a little bit. I would hear him, even if I was dead asleep, and give him some milk. He'd dream-feed for five or ten minutes and fall promptly back to sleep. But this time, he opened his eyes, rolled over, and said, *"Ah?"* which was baby language for "Time to play?"

This didn't bode well for me. "Ah?" could mean I might be up for another hour or two. Kingston lay on his tummy, waiting for my reply. The room was very bright that night. We could see each clearly by the light filtering through the French doors from the backyard. I watched him watching me, like an old West standoff. *What is he looking at?* I wondered. *What does he see?*

Kingston wiggled over, trying to get as close to me as possible while he talked softly in the dark. He patted my neck with his hands and wiggled his body up on top of mine until he was nose to nose with me. He then took the opportunity to drool a long, pearly strand of saliva right down into the corner of my eye. This accomplished, he plopped his head forward onto my cheek.

"On no," I whispered into his ear. "The baby's trying to eat me again. Don't eat me, Baby. Who's going to take care of you in the morning if you gnaw Mama's face off? That would be unsightly."

I rolled him back over, patting his tummy. Luckily, his eyes began to flicker shut. He struggled to keep them open but he was losing the battle and I was winning. Kingston held on to my hand with his two tiny ones, halfheartedly gnawing on one of my knuckles. Within a couple of minutes he was knocked out again. I wrapped myself up like a blanket around him and finally fell asleep.

The next morning was a Saturday. We all got up and tried to decide what to do with our one day of family time.

"We could go to the beach," I said to Cory, then thought better of it. "Nah, too cold."

The weather was supposed to be a nippy 73 degrees.

"We could go back to the park," I suggested.

"Yeah," Cory said. "But what would we do after?"

"How about we go for a drive up the coast?"

"That might be fun," Cory agreed. "We could head up to Topanga Canyon and look at the horses. King might like to see some horses today. What do you think, little man?"

Kingston blew himself a beard full of spit bubbles, the highest form of baby enthusiasm.

"Sounds like a plan," I said. "Let's get dressed—"

Before I could finish the sentence, my phone chimed. I was kind of curious about who'd be calling this early on a Saturday, but I didn't necessarily want to answer the phone. So I dawdled on my way toward the coffee table, stopping at the refrigerator to look for juice. Then I headed around through the dining room to the living room. Shockingly, by the time I made it to the coffee table my cell phone had stopped ringing. Oh well. Maybe next time.

"I guess they'll have to call back," I said. "By the way, I have to do a little more on that Fu-Gen report I was working on. If I can e-mail it to them before we leave I'll be free for the rest of the day."

"Okay," Cory said. "We'll walk to Simply Wholesome for some breakfast. By the time we get food and come back you should be done."

"Let's do it."

Just as Cory and Kingston walked out the door, my phone buzzed with a new text. What now? I walked over and picked it up, curious about what could be so important at the God-awful hour of 9:00 a.m. on a Saturday. It was a message from Lisa.

He left me. It's over. Please call.

Lisa and her husband were one of the happiest couples we knew. I'm sure they had their issues like everyone else. But they were united, a team. When other couples were dropping like flies, they had seemed inseparable. I immediately thought about their children, ten-year-old Michelle and eight-year-old Darren. A divorce would be devastating. I called back immediately.

"What happened?"

Lisa was in tears.

"Glenn said that he fell in love with my best friend and it's over."

"What?"

"I asked him how he could do something like this and he wouldn't say anything more. So I confronted her about it."

"What did she say?"

"She claimed that nothing had ever happened between the two of them. She said he was crazy. Apparently he feels strongly enough about her to end our fifteen-year marriage, but she claims she wants nothing to do with him and she doesn't know what he's talking about. So I don't know what's going on."

I tried as hard as I could to say something to ease her pain. But I couldn't think of anything. I felt helpless.

"It's really over," she cried.

"Hey," I said. "Are you busy? We'd love to come over and see you today."

Lisa sniffled. "Okay."

She sounded relieved to have someone to be with.

"We're getting dressed," I said. "We're on our way."

Forty minutes later, we were headed down the 10 freeway.

"I don't get it," I said to Cory as we turned onto the 110 freeway, racing past downtown Los Angeles, headed east toward Mt. Washington. "This doesn't make any sense."

Cory just shook his head. "Don't look at me. I don't know either. Things just happen sometimes."

He seemed a lot calmer than I would've thought he'd be.

"What are you talking about? They have two kids. These things don't just happen. Nobody sprinkles breakup pixie dust over you at night and all of a sudden you wake up in the morning and end your marriage. People let these things happen. They *make* them happen. But why?"

"Sometimes people aren't compatible."

"Why would you say that?"

Cory sighed. "I just can't say that I'm surprised. I don't think their dynamic was sustainable over the long haul. It just seemed like, from the outside looking in, Lisa was more of a mother than a wife. She ran the show. That kind of thing will last for a while, but it's ultimately unhealthy for both people."

It takes two, I thought. *You can't have a mother unless you have a child.* But I kept my mouth shut. We just drove along in silence for the last few minutes. As Cory pulled into their driveway, Michelle and Darren ran out to greet us.

"Hi, Uncle Cory," they said in unison. "Hi, Auntie Kuwana. Hi, Kingston."

The baby squealed at the children, whom he adored.

"Hey," Cory said. "Why don't we go inside and take the baby upstairs and play?"

Lisa was sitting on the couch in the middle of the living room with the blackout shades drawn. The kids scurried quietly past her up the stairs, with Cory and the baby trailing behind.

As soon as they were out of sight, I sat down and asked, "What happened?"

"I don't know," Lisa whispered. "I don't even know where to begin. He was just tired of being married, I guess."

"What's going on with this woman? Who is she?"

Lisa's face tightened. "She's one of my best friends. Or at least she was. Her children are two of Michelle and Darren's best friends. They see each other all the time at school. I can't believe he was selfish enough to do something like this without taking all that into consideration."

"Were they really having an affair? It doesn't sound like it."

"Well, according to them, they're not having an affair. But he's decided that he's in love with her and he wants to pursue a relationship with her. Our marriage is in the way of that because, of course, the new relationship can't happen as long as she and I are still friends and he and I are still married."

"So he's initiated this breakup because he wants to have a relationship with someone who's already said that she wants no part of him?"

"You got it."

"No, I don't buy it. There's more to it than that."

Lisa sighed. "We've had some rough patches over the last year or so and I think the truth is that he doesn't want to deal with it anymore. I keep asking him to grow up and to take his share of the responsibility and he keeps saying yes, yes, yes and then just doesn't do it."

Lisa had reframed the mother–child dysfunction dynamic that Cory had been talking about, except she described it from the mother's perspective. Very interesting.

"Are you going to go to counseling before you just end it?"

"I asked him to go to counseling and he said he would, but at the same time he's been trolling Internet dating sites."

"Oh, come on. How do you know for sure that he's been on dating sites?"

"Because the dumb-ass used my credit card to sign up for them! He doesn't have any money. He uses my money. I told you, he's a child."

I had to take a moment to recoup from that one.

"Yeah, that would make it a little bit harder," I mumbled. I was hoping to be a voice of reason, but Glenn sure hadn't left me much to work with.

"He always complains that I take charge of everything," Lisa said. "But then, at the same time, he refuses to step up. I begged him to be part of the decision making in the house, and he wouldn't. But when he didn't like the decisions I made, he'd tell me how unhappy he was and that it was all my fault. It's literally the same conversation I have with my eight-year-old. I don't call Glenn a kid to be spiteful. I truly believe he was stunted in his childhood. He never grew up. And then he puts his mommy issues off on me, instead of dealing with the problems that we have on the table now, as two adults. Honestly, I'm sick of it too. Instead of acting out with me, he needs to just tell his real mother that he's angry. That man has forty years' worth of repressed anger. Maybe if he acknowledged it to her, he could move on with the rest of his life."

"Why do you think he takes those issues out on you?"

Lisa sighed. "Glenn never learned how to express himself or ask for what he needs. But he'll turn around and complain that everybody else is manipulating him because that's how he was treated in the past. When he gets upset, he immediately goes to this space of blame, where all these different people have done him wrong. He's stuck and there's nothing I can do with that. I can't fight ghosts."

"What's his mother's side of the story? Have you all ever talked it out?"

"Do you know what my relationship with Phyllis has been like? Let me tell you a story that happened before Glenn and I got married."

Lisa shifted her weight on the couch, pulling her shirt down over her stomach.

"I know I'm not what Phyllis expected in a daughter-in-law," she said. "I'm fat. I get that. I have dark skin, and I don't think she was prepared for that either. I wasn't the aesthetic that she was used to. Phyllis was a slender, fair-skinned beauty queen. Her children were handsome. Glenn's girl-friend before me was Miss USA. Phyllis and her mother were the crème de la crème of society back in the day. When Glenn and I first got together, they were horrified and they didn't even try to hide it. It didn't matter how smart or talented I was, or that I was a good person—I wasn't good enough.

"Well, right before we got married, Phyllis and her mother, Jane, took Glenn and me out to lunch. I thought they were trying make amends so we could start learning how to get along. But you know what happened? We met up at a swank restaurant in Beverly Hills. As a matter of fact, Eddie Murphy and Sugar Ray Leonard were having lunch at the table next to us. I was all excited that we were going to talk and really get to know each other so that we could put the past behind us and I could be part of the family. I wanted them to like me.

"We had barely sat down at the table when Jane turned to me and said, 'You are not good enough for my grandson!' I was horrified. Then Phyllis says, 'We really don't think you should get married. You're so young and there's no need to rush things. We want you to rethink this and call off the wedding. It's selfish. I understand that right now you're only concerned with yourselves. But, my God, think about the other people involved. I mean have you ever considered what your children would look like?' Then they both stood up and walked away.

"And do you want to hear the worst part? At that moment, Eddie Murphy turns around to me and says, 'Oh man! That was cold!' Then he turns to Sugar Ray and says, 'Did you hear that? That was just cold! They didn't have no right to do her like that!' Then he turns to the people across the way and says, 'Oh, man! Now, y'all know that was cold!' So, if there was anybody in the room who hadn't been paying attention, they were clearly involved now. I wanted to crawl into a hole. Not only had they clowned me, they clowned me in front of a whole room full of strangers who didn't even know me. How can you dislike someone that much? And that was just the beginning."

Before she could finish, Cory came back downstairs with the kids. Lisa wiped her face and put on a smile for them. They smiled back, but their hearts were heavy. I could see it. They were stressed out. I tried not to stare, but I almost couldn't help it. Their little faces seemed to have aged overnight.

For the rest of the after-noon and all the way home that evening, I kept seeing that look on their faces. I kept hearing the pain in Lisa's

> It made me wonder: How much influence do mothers really have over their children?

voice, the anger at her husband. I kept hearing her mumble, "Fourteen years... Fourteen years..." under her breath when she thought no one was listening. How could Glenn be so caught up in the past that he'd willingly destroy his relation-ships in the present? Was it all just an excuse, or was Glenn really acting out forty years' worth of repression and misery? I thought about Phyllis, whom I knew quite well. She seemed to have good intentions most of the time. And she obviously loved her sons and her grandchildren. What went wrong?

We drove past the tall, shimmering buildings downtown as the sun set over the ocean in the distance. The reflection of the orange sun against the glass made it look like the build-ings were ablaze. Buildings burning, sun setting—my mind was being pulled toward endings.

I could hear Kingston gurgling and squirming in his car seat. It made me wonder: How much influence do mothers really have over their children? Would Kingston be reliving some mistake that I made forty years from now?

I'd read certain articles which claimed that parents have little or no influence over their children beyond providing the genetic material to make them. According to this worldview people's beliefs, habits, and traits come mainly from their peers, their cohort group, and the society into which they're born. The influence of parents is minimal at best.

The other end of the spectrum says that caregivers are the ultimate influence over their children. In fact, new discoveries in the field of epigenetics have revealed that experiences during our formative years not only affect our emotional compass, but can trigger changes in the epigenomes of our very DNA. For example, the quality and responsiveness of mothering that a baby girl receives can turn on—or turn off—the genes linked to her own ability to mother later in her life. These changes can even be passed down, effectively altering the DNA of our children's children.

In other words, your mother did it.

No, that's not what the researchers were getting at, but talk about a head trip.

The idea of having that kind of power over someone else made me feel slightly queasy. It made me think, What exactly was I teaching my son? It can be so easy to go on autopilot as a parent, not to think about how your actions are informing your children. How wide their little eyes really are. When my son looked at me and looked at the life that I was living, even as young as he was, what was he seeing? Was he seeing me? Or was he seeing a retooled version of my mother and her choices? For the first time, I really thought about that question and had to admit that there was much more of my mother's spirit active and alive in me than I'd ever realized.

My mother was a survivor. She overcame poverty and lack

> When you numb your fear, or self-medicate in any way, you also end up numbing your joy, your ability to experience the sublime emotions, and the ability to connect.

of education and addiction and violence to try to build some sort of a life for me and my brother. No matter what happened, no matter how overwhelmed or ill-equipped she might have felt, she always got up every morning and she kept going. I became a survivor just like my mother. No matter what, I learned to just keep going. I learned to put one foot in front of the other and to never, ever give up. I took that lesson well.

Growing up, it didn't faze me to carry a knife or that I had other friends who carried razor blades and guns. It didn't matter that so many of the kids around our neighborhood were being killed, or killing each other, or that you could hear semiautomatics going off intermittently all night long during the hot summer months. I was sure that I could survive that.

Being able to put your head down and power through life had definite advantages. However, I'd found that there were two problems with that way of being. The first problem was that living in survival mode leads you to become emotionally numb. As psychologist Dr. Brenée Brown has poignantly explained, when we get into the practice of numbing one set of emotions we, by default, numb all emotions. In other words, you can't just numb fear while keeping exhilaration and power. When you numb your fear, or self-medicate in any way, you also end up numbing your joy, your ability to experience the sublime emotions, and the ability to connect.

The other problem is that surviving doesn't leave any room for thriving. To survive, by definition, means just getting by. When we seek to thrive, on the other hand, life becomes a playground. There are surprises around every corner. Some might be scary. Some might be amazing. But no matter what, you recognize life as something to be embraced with openheartedness and courage, to be lived from a space of wholeness rather than from a fractured, piecemeal identity. Rather than keeping our heads down to avert the grinding heel of life, we shine.

I wanted to shine, to see my life through this new perspective. I wanted to release my old beliefs, which routinely clouded my view. Acknowledging something like this is hard enough when you're talking about yourself and your own growth. But how, I wondered, do you take on the responsibility of teaching someone else lessons and principles that you have not yet mastered for yourself?

We pulled into our driveway and Cory jumped out of the car. He opened my door first and went around to open the door on the baby's side. I walked around the back of the car and reached inside to unhook Kingston's buckle. The baby was drowsy. His eyes were red and his long lashes brushed against his cheeks every time his eyelids slipped shut. But then they'd pop back open, searching for me. Even in that half-conscious state, he knew I was close by.

"Come on, sweet boy," I whispered. "Let's go inside and get you ready for bed."

I cradled the baby against my chest as we walked straight to the back of the house. We stopped in his room long enough to pull a onesie out of his dresser.

"It's time for you to go night-night, my love," I sang in his ear. "Sleepy, sleepy baby, Mama loves you."

I tried to lay Kingston down in the bed, but he wouldn't let go of my hand.

"It's okay, sweetheart. I'm just going to get a new diapy for you, that's all."

I slipped free from his little fingers and walked the three steps to the changing table. He whined and fretted the entire time, his eyes following me as he rolled over from his back onto his tummy, trying to wiggle his way toward me.

"Stay still, little baby," I said. "I'm not going anywhere."

The fact that he wouldn't let me out of his sight wasn't lost on me, in light of what we'd been talking about all afternoon. I picked my son back up and held him close to my heartbeat, letting him know that he was safe. He was so precious. So trusting. I was reminded of something a good friend had told me one afternoon: "He looks to you for everything. You are his higher self."

The baby stared up at me with such open, innocent eyes that I was suddenly overcome by tears. I felt so grateful and so full. I didn't quite know how to receive this heartbreaking gift. This kind of love felt almost unbearable. I hoped that one day I'd be able to hold this depth of love with grace. I prayed that it wouldn't feel so powerful and consuming to be broken open this way. Standing in front of the bedroom doors, rocking back and forth with the baby in my arms, I could look outside and see an entirely new sky, an entirely new moon. I could see the trees colored blue in the moonlight, with the pruned branches propped up against the night. People, like trees, must also be pruned, I knew. The old, dead things must be stripped away so that

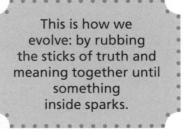

This is how we evolve: by rubbing the sticks of truth and meaning together until something inside sparks.

what is new can have room to flourish. But unlike the trees, the old beliefs and lessons in my mind couldn't be pruned by someone else. If I was living with things that no longer served me, it was my responsibility to lay them down.

I'd walked through much pain on my path to finding the beauty within me. But, as always, the pain was simply an indicator that I was moving through the death of what hadn't worked and being birthed into something that could work for my growth and evolution. In the same way, it was painful allowing Kingston into the world. He had to be pushed out. He didn't just fly through the birth canal, arriving magically in my arms. He was massaged and squeezed and molded and pushed until he came.

We're all molded this way by life, by our families, our experiences, and our perceptions. We assign meaning to all of it, whether that meaning has merit or merely history behind it. This is how we evolve: by rubbing the sticks of truth and meaning together until something inside sparks. When we stay stuck in the past—stuck in blame, fear, and false beliefs—the fire inside stays unlit. Life is small and cold.

I was aware of being stoked into something infinitely bigger, more expansive, and wiser than I was able to grasp at the moment. And that was fine. Because my only job was to recognize that it was happening and stay open to the process. I could not, under any circumstances, let my heart close again. For this understanding I was grateful.

I nursed our son to sleep contemplating the idea that the gratitude in my heart could be a feeling that passed through or a habit that I cultivated. The feeling of gratitude disappears when something doesn't pan out the "right" way. It will also disappear when people don't do what you think they should do or what you want them to do. It becomes easy to blame others—our parents, our spouses, our children—for not living up to the goals and expectations that we assign them, or for stopping us from achieving our own. That is a recipe for a life of misery. It robs us of responsibility for ourselves and our choices and prevents us from seeing what is in front of us.

The habit of gratitude begins with knowing that if anything had been any different in our lives up to this moment, we would not be who we are today. Who we are is absolutely perfect and necessary to move into who we can be tomorrow. Most importantly, it allows us the space to stand in the embodiment of our truth right now. Our children thrive in the now. Possibility exists in the now. The healing of the generations that have written their stories on my face can only happen through me right now.

I could write a million words and travel to every continent, but the first, most important step of that journey would be to travel within, and write out a million words of love and forgiveness and gratitude on my own heart. That is what Kingston will grow up reading. I prayed that this would be my part of the legacy that would shape the face of the man he will become. Anything else he can just let go.

Soul Mates and the Language of Inspired Loving

If everybody likes you, you're lying to some-one.

—GRANDMA

TRYING TO BE ALL THINGS TO ALL PEOPLE AT ALL TIMES really isn't very much fun. Believe it or not, after a while it takes its toll.

We were packing to go back to the East Coast because Cory had a court date with my friend Francis, whom we were suing for the return of our car or the money to reimburse us for it. The past year and a half had been full of promises, half-truths, outright lies, and excuses. Now we were down to our last resort option.

A court date wasn't the best reason to fly all the way across the country lugging the baby with you—a baby who had never even worn shoes, much less experienced a real East Coast winter. Between getting our paperwork together, packing our clothes, deciding which toys and books to take on the plane, calling friends back home, checking up on Lisa, and trying to get a little bit more work done before we left, I felt so overwhelmed I didn't know which way to turn.

Everywhere I looked all I could see was another task that had to be done on time. I rummaged through my closet looking for clothes that could stand up against the late-winter frost, pulling random things off hangers and throwing them down in the corner when they weren't what I actually wanted.

With the baby strapped against my chest, we scuttled through the house picking up this, discarding that, both of us pulling on my hair in frustration. Turning back to the closet again, I grabbed a heavy sweater from a hanger and dropped it into my "keep" pile. As I did so, my towering "no way" pile toppled over onto the first pile, making another mountain of mess. Before I could scream, the voice in my head said, *Embrace the confusion and the activity in the same way you embrace your son.*

I looked down at Kingston and he looked up at me. Then he grabbed my lower lip and pulled for all he was worth.

"Hey, naughty baby!"

Kingston laughed and gave me his scrunchy-nose mischief face.

"Are you trying to tell Mama to stop poking her lip out? Fine. Point taken."

Kingston never failed to get straight to the point. There was nothing cryptic or mystical about his communication.

Cory's father, Willie, picked us up that evening just as the sun was setting and drove us to LAX. We went through security pretty easily and checked in at our gate. The baby wanted to see everything and touch everything and eat everything in sight. Even though it was getting on toward bedtime, he didn't seem the least bit sleepy. I hoped he would fall asleep on the plane, but seeing as this was his first flight, I had no idea what to expect.

We boarded the plane and, much to my delight, Kingston

loved it. He called out in his singsong voice to the people sitting in front of us and then, just in case the people behind us felt neglected, he spoke with them too. The flight

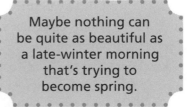

Maybe nothing can be quite as beautiful as a late-winter morning that's trying to become spring.

attendants were smitten. It was official. The airplane was a hit. Shortly after takeoff, Kingston settled down to nurse and was fast asleep within minutes. He stirred only once during the five-hour flight. But I nursed him again and he drifted peacefully back to sleep.

When we landed in Virginia, the other passengers gave us the highest compliment that single people can give parents traveling with an infant: "I didn't even know you had a baby sitting there! What a wonderful child!" This, of course, is singleton code for "Thank God he didn't keep me up all night or we would've been fighting!" I was feeling kind of chipper and upbeat myself because I was finally back on my side of the world. It was good to be home. Almost home, anyway.

The sun rose as we bumped along in the airport shuttle toward one of the rental car buildings. At once, Kingston was wide awake. Sunshine meant *Get up, time to play!* That was a universal definition, regardless of which time zone we were in. Playtime was as immutable as the elements. Cory bounced the baby and kissed his red cheeks while I watched the sky fill with cold orange light. Maybe nothing can be quite as beautiful as a late-winter morning that's trying to become spring. I couldn't wait to see all my old friends. Before the court date, we'd have time to hang out for a night with two of my best friends who lived in town. I'd known Tiffany and Towanda since the fifth grade. They couldn't have been more different. Yet, at the same time, we all had so much in common. We'd come from the same place.

Cory, Kingston, and I got our car and began the three-hour drive down to Hampton. Kingston, who was still no fan of the car seat, was surprisingly cooperative. Meaning that he didn't scream our ears bloody for at least two hours before dropping into an exhausted stupor. We were staying with my mother-in-law's friend Ondrej. When we finally arrived at Ondrej's house, she immediately made us welcome. She fussed over us all as though we were her family. This was what I missed about being at home, about being with my people—even though technically she was Cory's people by way of his mother. But the affection was the same; it was a feeling of connection and ease.

After a shower and a nap, we headed out for an early dinner with my friend Towanda and her family and my friend Tiffany and her on-again, off-again boyfriend Rob. I'd been hearing about Rob since we were in high school. Somehow he and Tiffany were still together. Sort of. After twenty years of Rob stories, I was so excited to actually meet him. It was like finally seeing one of the teachers in the "Charlie Brown" cartoons. You get to lay eyes on someone who's only existed as a story line in your imagination.

We walked into the restaurant and I saw them almost immediately. My friends. Back together again, it was like no time had passed. Towanda, her husband, Gilbert, her daughter, and her son were there, along with her brother Abraham and his family. This was the first time that they were meeting Cory, and Tiffany was especially full of stories to tell Cory about all the crazy things I used to do.

"Oh, KK, you didn't tell Cory about that?" she'd say. "Girl, you know that story is too juicy! Cory, listen to this…"

Tiffany was a high school teacher, which made perfect sense. She loved to talk and being a teacher meant she had a captive audience all day long.

"Tell me more. I want to know what Kuwana was like as a kid," Cory said.

The laughter was uproarious. They laughed a little too loud, if you asked me, while they filled Cory in on stories of me as the mastermind of chaos. Admittedly, I was a bit of a handful when I was younger. I had a little too much imagination for my own good, maybe. That creativity might have expressed itself in some interesting ways. But then some big-mouthed person started talking about *the hamster episode*.

Cory looked at me and folded his arms over his chest. "Do I want to hear this one?"

"Probably not," I warned.

"Tell me anyway."

"Suffice it to say that one time, when we were about ten years old, I needed some hamster bones—"

"Bones?"

"Yes," I replied very coolly, like, *What ten-year-old doesn't need a few bones once in a while?* "And the hamster that we had at the time didn't want to give hers up."

"Should baby be hearing this?" Cory asked.

"There's nothing else for him to hear," I insisted. "That's the end of the story."

"No, it's not!" Towanda yelled. "Tell the truth and shame the devil."

"Fine. I wanted to do a diorama of an archaeological dig with a little archaeologist looking for dinosaur bones. My friend Haydee happened to have the bones of her old hamster in a glass jar. Cory, be quiet. Don't ask why. I don't know. Just let me finish the story. Unfortunately, my mother didn't see an award-winning science project when she looked at the bones. She saw a jar of crap and threw them out. So I had to get some new hamster bones real quick and switch them out so Haydee wouldn't know the difference. Towanda and I walked down Castle Hill Avenue to the pet store and bought a hamster. We took it home to her house and waited for it to die."

People were already snorting with laughter. I still didn't see the humor.

"The first few days came and went and nothing happened. So we decided to stop waiting for her to die and just play with her. Then, of course, that's when she croaked. So we took her downstairs to the laundry room, laid out some newspaper, and—"

Their disgusted cries drowned out the rest. But by then I was on a roll. This was starting to get fun.

"No, no, no, you wanted to hear about it. So we decide to go and dissect the hamster down in the laundry room."

"And somehow," Towanda said, "Abraham found us down there with a pair of scissors and a kitchen knife and started screaming that he was gonna tell my mother."

"And somehow that ended up with us chasing him around the living room and threatening him with a hamster leg until he promised not to tell," I concluded.

Everybody groaned.

"What?" I shrugged. "They make you dissect frogs in biology class. I figured it was going to be the same thing. It wasn't, but that's what I thought at the time."

"Did you tell your mother?" Cory asked Abraham.

I watched Towanda as her brother shook his head no. Her eyes closed for a brief moment and her shoulders slumped. It was just a slight movement, but its funny how you catch things when you really know someone. Their mother had passed away earlier that year and Towanda was still devastated. Shirley Slycott had been a pillar of the community and her daughter's best friend. Thinking back to the old times, the good days with our families intact and safe, was still hard. The joy of remembering was taking its toll.

"Hey, guys," I said, changing the subject. "Do you remember that time I flipped Abraham across the living room? I was taking a karate class and he didn't believe that I knew any karate and he kept telling me I couldn't flip him."

"Hold on! I don't know nothing about that," Abraham grumbled.

"Wait a minute, wait a minute!" his wife laughed. "I don't think I've ever heard this story."

"Well, he kept poking at me and poking at me until I grabbed his arm and flipped him over my shoulder. He flew across the back of the couch and rolled down onto the seat cushion—"

"—Off the couch and right through the glass coffee table," Towanda said.

"Oooooohhhh!" Everybody groaned.

"That must've hurt," Rob said, shaking his head.

"Yeah," I laughed. "I was banned from the house for a while after that one. Hey, Tiff, do you remember…"

With that, the conversation moved on to safer, charted waters. It was hard to see Towanda in pain. She wore her grief like an overcoat, wanting to take it off but not quite sure where to set it. That's what happens when you lose the ones you came to this world to find and to love. The threads of certainty and belonging that make up our web of connection get cut. It takes patience and faith to spin the web in a new pattern.

We talked and laughed and before we knew it, it was time to go. We were all adults with small children who had bedtimes. We were at the time in our lives when "late into the night" meant anytime after 8:30 p.m. As we made our way to our respective cars, I was filled with such gratitude for having experienced so much acceptance and love in my life. After all, you really have to love somebody to let them come back over after they've thrown you through a glass table.

The next morning, we got up early and traveled to the Chesapeake courthouse. Francis didn't even bother to show up on time. We had prepared piles and piles of paperwork and a whole timeline to try to describe the convoluted events that had brought us there. But in Francis's absence, the judge just struck the gavel and ruled in our favor. It was almost anticlimactic. I wondered where Francis could possibly be that was so important that he would miss his day in court. However, we found out from one of the court officers (whom Cory had befriended on the phone, because Cory befriends everyone) that Francis had dozens of lawsuits against him. One more wouldn't make a difference one way or the other. She showed us a printout of plaintiffs that, between Francis and his wife, spanned more than ten pages.

Unbelievable.

After fifteen years of friendship, all I was to him was another name on his list. Once the judge ruled in our favor, he instructed us to take our paperwork to the clerk's office. The clerks would begin processing the request to serve Francis with an order to pay more than $15,000.

As we waited for the clerks to complete their process, Francis showed up, dripping wet from the rain, rushing like he had someplace important to be. Unless somebody else was suing him right after us, which was possible, he had nowhere to go. The case was over. The window of opportunity had closed on his fingertips.

I glanced down the corridor and saw him closing in on us. My heart quickened. He walked over to my husband, who was standing about twenty feet away from me. Francis looked cold and overwhelmed and sorrowful. In spite of my anger, I began to feel sorry for him, the friend I'd lost. They talked for a few minutes, though I couldn't hear what was being said. Cory's jaw tightened up and his eyes narrowed. It was probably as close to rage as I had ever seen him come.

Francis shook Cory's hand, turned around slowly, and walked back the way he came. His shoulders were hunched and his head was lowered. A few minutes later, we also left the courthouse, wading back through the shin-deep puddles in the parking lot, trying to stay dry under our umbrella. I didn't ask what Francis had said or tell Cory how sad I felt, for fear that he'd never be able to understand. Very quietly, we gathered our belongings from Ondrej's house, packed the car, and moved on.

The rain stopped on our drive north. Unfortunately, the winter cold stepped up in full force to take its place. We arrived in DC shortly before my mother was scheduled to arrive by train at Union Station. She was too impatient to wait for us to make it all way back to New York, so she'd decided to meet us halfway. In the meantime, we checked into our hotel and got ready to head out and see the town. In celebration of being in DC, I parted the baby's hair on the side, slicked it back, and dressed him in a striped sweater vest and some khakis. Voilà! Senator Kingston. Then we walked to the Capitol and took pictures on the steps. Kingston looked adorable in his brand-new striped winter jumper with the pointed elf hood. It was the only wintery piece of clothing he had. After we finished playing, we walked through the cold back toward the train station. People charging down the sidewalks were as numerous as cars on the 405 freeway at rush hour in LA. This entranced Cory, who looked like any minute he might yell out, *Skyscrapers and everything!*

"All this history," he mused. "All the power plays, the wheeling and dealing... You can almost smell it in the air."

"That's bus fumes," I replied.

"See, there's your sardonic child self coming out. I recognize it now."

Maybe so.

We headed inside the enormous train station and made our way to my mother's arrival platform. It wasn't long before we heard her screaming, "Wanie!" Then I knew I was home.

• • •

The next day, we drove Cory back to the airport. He had to head home for work. I didn't realize how hard it would be to say good-bye to him until he was walking down the corridor toward his gate. We hadn't been apart since before we were engaged. I'd really grown accustomed to his unrelenting optimism. He's the kind of person who gets interviewed on radio shows and documentaries about positivity. Needless to say, he was harassed by me and my entire family almost from the word go. The fact that I was now missing all that California sunshine was a hard thing to admit for a sardonic born-and-bred New Yorker like myself.

But I shook it off and went back to the car. What else could I do? It was time to go.

"Everybody strapped in?"

"Yes," my mother answered.

"You ready too, Kingston?"

The baby gurgled fretfully from his car seat in the back. He sounded anxious. It was like he knew that his father was about to fly away, literally disappearing into the sunset like some old-timey western. Cory and Kingston had never been separated longer than the time it took for Cory to get to work in the morning and come home at night. I wondered how they'd adjust.

We eased into traffic and carefully made our way around toward I-95 North. The scenery was so familiar and at the same time so new. As we drove, Mommy talked and talked about the latest developments that had been going on since the last time I was home. A lot had happened to everyone. I hadn't been around for a while.

After visiting some more friends, we drove to Camden, New Jersey, to see my grandparents and my father. They'd never seen the baby, and time was running out for my father. He was dying of AIDS, and if he didn't meet the baby now he might not get another opportunity. I loved my father dearly. He had such a sweet nature, always ready to help anyone who looked like they needed a hand. He would build computers for poor families around Camden, mostly single mothers with school-aged children who couldn't afford to buy the late-model computers that the schools wanted the children to have. He was always ready with a story or game or poem by Robert Frost. A wasteful genius, he'd won presidential commendations and a Penn Award for his writing, though he'd long since given up the pen for the needle.

By this time, after so many years, he was very ill and unable to consistently take care of himself. He couldn't remember to take his meds on time, but he could meticulously list every pain and ailment that then *mysteriously* beset his body. Personally, I thought he was just biding his time.

We arrived at my grandparents' ramshackle house in Camden well after dark. Not the best time to be cruising through that town. My grandfather had always done such a good and conscientious job of keeping the place up. But he was getting older and didn't have much help. It showed in the sad posture of the old white house, which sagged just a bit. If the house had an expression, it would be a perpetual sigh. Walking up the little stone steps toward the front door, I almost wished that I lived closer. I wanted to help.

"Hey, hey, hey! Look who's here," Papa said, opening the screen door for us.

He hugged me tightly and kissed the baby. His rough

whiskers made Kingston laugh out loud. Then he embraced Mommy in a happy hug.

"Hey, Marge, look who's here!"

My grandmother shuffled through the living room toward us with her arms open wide.

"Come in, come in!"

"Hi Grammy," my mother beamed.

She'd always had such a warm relationship with my father's parents, probably because she hadn't been close to her own mother. I loved seeing them all together in that one little room, excited and happy. Papa trudged to the foot of the stairs and called up.

"James! James! Get down here," he yelled.

There was no answer. My grandfather started up the stairs but I jumped in front of him and said, "That's okay, Papa, you don't have to go back up. I'll go get him."

I took the baby's jacket off, laid it down on the couch, and then climbed the two flights of stairs into the attic where my father was resting.

"Look who's here," I said. Daddy turned over in his little bed so that he could see me from my place in the attic stairwell.

He grinned. "Hello, Ms. Wana." His voice was raspy and unused. He'd been asleep a long time. "And who is this you have here?"

"Someone came to meet you," I said, smiling. "Come on downstairs so we can talk."

I refused to bring the baby up into the cold, cluttered little attic. I didn't want my father up there either, but I didn't have a choice in the matter about that. Before he could protest, I had turned around and headed back down toward

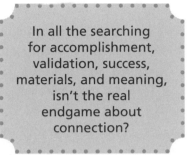

In all the searching for accomplishment, validation, success, materials, and meaning, isn't the real endgame about connection?

the living room. A few minutes later he appeared at the foot of the stairs. My parents hugged. They seemed genuinely happy to see each other, which was always nice. It didn't matter that I was thirty-six years old. Seeing my parents be kind to each other still made me feel safe and welcomed. Connected. And isn't that what I'd been after? Isn't that what everyone really wants?

In all the searching for accomplishment, validation, success, materials, and meaning, isn't the real endgame about connection? Cohesion. Integration. Aren't these the things that give life meaning, that bind us to one another, generation to generation? These are the things that grow the roots of our family trees. The deeper the roots, the straighter and taller the tree stands. The taller the tree, the higher and faster the birds that live in them can fly.

For many years, I had believed that the roots of my tree were gnarled and knotted; they didn't go deep enough into the earth to be sustaining. Watching my parents standing together with the baby between them made me begin to see our shared ecosystem a little differently. Perhaps our roots didn't go as deep as I might've liked, but they spread out wide, embracing everything.

I walked over and took the baby into my arms.

"Time for a diaper change."

We walked into the back bedroom carrying our red travel bag. My father followed. I took this as a very special opportunity. As much as I loved my father I also knew him quite well. He could disappear at any time. Our moments together were usually brief, so I tried to fill them up.

"So how are you, Daddy?"

"Oh, not bad. I have to have another operation on my shoulders soon. But I'm actually looking forward to that one. It should be interesting to see what they're going to do. I've got a team of the top specialists in the world working on my case."

"Oh, really? How did you manage that?"

"I have my ways," he said with a self-important smirk.

"That may be true, but what you don't have is money. So where are the doctors coming from?"

My father proceeded to tell me how he wrangled these renowned doctors in Philadelphia into taking on his case. Under other circumstances, that wouldn't have been hard to believe. My father was a very articulate man. He was one of the smartest people I knew. How he was able to continue to do advanced mathematics and put together entire computer systems with nothing more than a few screwdrivers and some salvaged parts, all while being high on heroin, I couldn't understand. He just did it.

But then, just as I was starting to believe him, he launched into a whole discourse about alien spaceships and abductions. Then he made a choppy segue into a story about having traveled to Japan with a friend, giving detailed and soaring accounts of his many exploits. I listened quietly, even though I knew that he'd never been out of the country.

I held the baby close, a shield over my heart, trying to figure out if my father was becoming unstable because of his meds or because of the drugs. Or was he simply trying to fill up his memories in ways that he hadn't been able to fill up his life? I couldn't tell. It didn't matter. I would take the last leg of the journey with him wherever it led. That's just what you do when you love someone. My father was a soul mate in the truest sense.

I've sometimes wondered if you can hate your soul mate. The answer is: of course. Only Hollywood says otherwise. We're told that soul mates come wrapped up in a glittery box with a big pink bow. When you open the box, rainbows of love and passion and ecstasy shoot forth. Only one person in the whole universe can give you this gift and if you lose it, woe unto you! You'll be a miserable, lonely wretch forever.

That's absolute crap.

The truth is, our soul mates are those who connect us to the depths and the heights of who and what we really are. They are those who love us enough, spirit to spirit, to ensure

> The truth is, our soul mates are those who connect us to the depths and the heights of who and what we really are.

that we're given everything we need to grow and unfold in this life. Sometimes that looks like bows and glitter and rainbows. Sometimes it looks like drug addiction. It's all the same. My father was my soul mate as much as my son. The difference was that I knew that my son has traveled a long and deliberate road to make it here to me and I welcomed every day with him as a celebration of his fortitude and his desire to be here, with us, in love.

My father did not choose a path that afforded him that kind of consciousness. Over the years I had to learn to find beauty in the path that he laid for both of us. And it has been beautiful, particularly getting to step into the role of parent. One of the greatest beauties of becoming a parent yourself is that you constantly have your stuff thrown up into your face. Rather than being perpetually horrified, I was beginning to realize that the resurgences of lingering pains were poignant opportunities to re-parent myself, to do it better, to lead my heart down a different road and in a new direction.

My mother and I stayed for two days before getting back on the road and traveling the last two hours to the city. My grandparents, my brother, my two sisters, my nieces, nephews, and the family dog, Tiger, all waved us off. We drove past boarded-up row houses down the narrow, pockmarked streets with the Philadelphia skyline rising in the background, sailing along on the highway toward home.

• • •

The truth is, we feel alive when we're connected

The next two weeks were a blur of activity. Everyone wanted to see the baby. Kingston loved traveling. He was so open and pliable everywhere we went. The strange faces and buildings and trains and buses and cars were all brand-new playthings for his mind. As long as I was there, he was thrilled to be on this adventure. I was his touchstone. Driving up the Whitestone Expressway to yet another relative's house, it hit me that all this time I'd been searching for the same thing: a touchstone. I wanted an anchor to hold me steady. There was so much new information to synthesize—about myself, the baby, people and relationships, desires, and my place in the middle of it all.

Kingston understood belonging. That understanding, in whatever ways babies process their reality, seemed to give him peace. He knew that he belonged with me—not to me, but with me. Big difference. Where did I belong? And with whom?

The truth is, we feel alive when we're connected, dead when we're not. The people and places that we love connect us to them and to ourselves like synapses, creating paths toward our greatest growth. When we get to the end of a certain path it's up to us to jump into the gap, trusting that we'll come out fine on the other side.

Sometimes this process feels amazing, sometimes not. But when laid end-to-end, the touchstones create a bridge to our greatest potential. I was lucky to have Kingston. He was definitely that bridge for me. He encouraged me every day to become a bridge into possibility for myself.

No, You Will Not Find Peace: Learning to Let Peace Find You

I know that God will never give me more than I can handle. I just wish he didn't trust me so much.

—MOTHER TERESA

WE'D SPENT ALMOST THREE WEEKS AT HOME WITH MY family—three wonderful, exhausting, frustrating weeks. Kingston and I were scheduled to fly out of Virginia again. So we packed up the car, said good-bye to my mother, and headed down I-95 toward the George Washington Bridge. The tenements lining the dingy highway seemed to hover over us like scolding relatives, watchful and disapproving. On our left the Manhattan skyline came into view. Watching the skyline appear and then disappear in my rearview mirror used to make me giddy: what would come next? Lately, the sight made me sad. But I also felt very strong and very proud then, especially knowing that my son was a part of my legacy now too.

Kingston sang along to his *Baby Loves Jazz* CD from the backseat. *Miles the Crocodile sings jazz colors for you! A wee wah, a wee wah a rooty toot toot!* It was great fun for the first twenty-five minutes. Unfortunately, we had two more hours to go until we reached South Jersey. By the time we arrived in Camden, the sun was setting and the baby was cranky. He hadn't fallen asleep and he wanted to make sure that I knew it.

"Mama, mama, mama, mama, ahhh mama!" he scream-ed.

He'd been saying "dada" and "nana" for months. He'd just gotten around to "mama," though he hadn't quite associated me with the word yet. He just liked yelling it. But I could see the little tumblers in his mind clicking as he realized that every time he sang, "Mama!" I perked up and said, "Yes!" I could see him realizing that whatever this new information meant, it would definitely come in handy for him later.

We got out of the car and trudged up a short flight of stairs to my grandparents' front door. Just like clockwork, my grandfather was standing there waiting.

"Well, hello! Look who's here! Hey, Marge—"

"Hi guys," I called out.

"Where's that baby?" my grandmother called back.

Kingston squealed in response. He loved being acknowledged first. Luckily for him, that was never a problem. My grandfather and I walked into the living room, dragging my luggage behind us. I brought the baby over to my grandmother, who was sitting in her La-Z-Boy chair. It wasn't easy for her to get around anymore because she'd had knee surgery. The recovery process was extremely slow and painful. The doctors wanted her to have surgery on the other knee, but she balked.

"Are they gonna help me up and down the stairs? I don't think so," she'd quipped. But the day was fast coming. It had to. Meanwhile, she spent most of her time seated at the kitchen table, on the couch, or in her chair. It hurt to see her being forced to slow down. But my grandmother was never one to ask for or tolerate pity.

My sister's four-year-old twins, Imani and Amir, were at the house when we arrived. They'd come over to see their Papa. Those two were just like me when I was growing up; Papa was their hero. They couldn't go more than a day or two without spending the night with Papa. So between the twins, Kingston, and Tiger, the monstrosity of a dog who careened around the living room pummeling people with his huge tail, we turned the house into a rowdy circus tent in a matter of minutes.

"Hey, Grammy," I said. "Where's Dad?"

"Oh, he went out for a while. I'm not sure where. I guess he'll be back sometime this evening."

That was disappointing. Not surprising, but disappointing.

My phone began to chime. Kingston was on the floor doing his army crawl toward Amir. Papa was dragging the dog into the kitchen so that he couldn't trample on the babies in his excitement. Tiger started barking like crazy, distraught at being left out of all that good playtime. Every time the dog barked, Kingston squealed with laughter. Not only did the huge, hairy dog *not* frighten Kingston, he seemed to believe that Tiger had appeared for his own personal amusement, like the slobbery clown in our bootleg circus. All was well. I took this as an opportunity to steal a quick phone call.

"Grammy, I'll be right back."

"Okay," she replied.

I walked a few feet away into the spare room off the living room, sat down on the bed, and hit the touch screen on my phone.

"Hey, babe," I said. "How are you?"

Cory sighed. Then he said, "I'm doing good."

"OK, what's up?"

"There's just a lot going on here. But I know it's all working out for our best and highest."

That meant there was really big trouble at home.

"What happened?"

"We have to move."

I sat there in silence for a moment, waiting for him to say something else. But he didn't.

"What do you mean?" I finally asked. "Why do we have to move?"

"Apparently, Marv was about to go into foreclosure on our house and to avoid that he put the house up for short sale. Someone bought it."

"When were we going to find out about this?"

"Now."

Obviously. My brain started bubbling. If Marv, the property owner, was in trouble, why hadn't he just said so? Hell, he could have asked us if we wanted to buy the property. He knew we were interested. Why couldn't anything ever be easy?

"The deal is final?"

"Apparently so," Cory said.

"When do we have to leave?"

"The end of the month."

"Which month?"

"The end of this coming month. Our thirty-day notice starts April first and we have to be out by May first."

We sat in silence for a long time.

"Where are we going to go?" I asked.

"I don't know," Cory said. "I'll find us something. It'll be all right."

I was long past the point in life where I could be brought to tears over material things, but I sure did feel like crying at that moment. All I could think of was the baby. We were going to have to uproot him from the only home he'd ever known. That thought made me panic. The more I tried not to panic, the more panicked I felt. What about his clothes, his toys, his room? What about the countertop in the kitchen where we gave him his first bath? What about the backyard where he'd first felt the grass under his feet and jumped into my arms laughing because it tickled him? What about Donna and Cecilia's dogs next door, who barked every time we came outside? They were annoying, complaining pit bulls. But Kingston didn't know that. He thought they were making friendly conversation. He made it a point to talk back each day, just to be neighborly.

Where would we go?

Cory said again, "We'll figure it out."

Had I been speaking out loud? I didn't think so, but I wasn't sure. Up until then, when I thought about going home the most pressing thing in my mind had been figuring out how many pages I'd be able to get done on my book. Now the novel was the last thing on my agenda. Now I didn't know when, or if, I'd be getting back to it. It's so amazing how fast and how completely life can change up on you.

We sat on the phone, commiserating in silence. I took deep breaths and tried to empty my mind. Clarity always helps to dispel fear. But it wasn't working. *I should be able to do at least that*, I fumed at myself. *It shouldn't be so hard. What's wrong with me?*

"Hey, I have to run back into the living room and get the baby. I'll try to call you later tonight after he goes to sleep."

"Okay, I'll talk to you then. Love you, babe. Bye."

I threw the phone down onto the bed, then picked it up and threw it down again. Why are things never just easy? I walked back into the 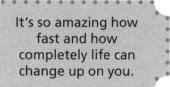 living room and looked down at the twins rolling around on the carpet. Kingston squealed, trying as best he could to keep up with them. At least Kingston was still having an easy-breezy time. What would it be like to be as carefree as him? How simple life would be.

"What's up, Ms. Wana?" Papa asked.

"Oh nothing," I lied. "Just tired."

No use burdening my grandparents with my cross-country dramas. Actually, there was no use burdening myself. There was nothing I could do about it now. I might as well just enjoy the rest of the trip and worry about it later. This seemed like the smart alternative. But no matter how calm I appeared on the outside, inside I felt frazzled and rushed and confused and angry. Consequently, everything around me began to mirror the state of my mind.

When my brother James came home from work, I asked him if he wanted to take a Dunkin' Donuts run—to which, of course, he said yes. But I couldn't get the car seat back in the car properly. It was loose and wobbly.

"Why won't this stupid thing work?" I slapped it around a couple of times, but the car seat was not intimidated.

My sister tried to fix it, then my brother tried, then I tried again. It got tighter, but it still wasn't right. I was beside myself with images of unavoidable calamity. What was going to happen when we had to get back on the road to Virginia and the airport tomorrow? What if we had a car crash the one time the car seat wasn't 100 percent reliable? On top of that, it looked like it might rain overnight and into the next day. A sharp, cold wind was blowing in off the water. We could skid out on some late-season ice patches tomorrow on the way down I-95. Highly unlikely in the beginning of April, but it could happen.

This was the thought process my mind went through all evening. Not even Dunkin' Donuts could fix it. I called it quits on the sugar run and begged off for the night, telling everyone that we were very sleepy and had a long day ahead of us. That part was true. We had a two- or three-hour drive to complete before fighting our way through the airport, waiting for another hour or two, and then taking a six-hour flight across the country. Did I mention the seven-and-a-half-month-old baby who was somehow supposed to sit patiently through all this?

I needed some rest.

Once Kingston was ready for bed I cradled him, walking him around in the darkened room and singing his favorite song gently in his ear. *Mama loves you, Daddy loves you, yes we do, yes we do. Mom and Daddy love you. Mom and Daddy love you. Love, love, love.*

He fell asleep easily, much to my surprise, with a lingering smile on his little lips. His cheek was pressed against my chest and I imagined that he could hear my heartbeat, a sound as familiar to him, as intimate, as his own breathing. He sighed and flung his little arm over his eyes. It was the same motion that Cory always did when he tried to sleep (or pretend to sleep) while I peppered him with my late-night insights and revelations. It's amazing how our children resemble us in these unexpected ways. Almost as amazing as the ways in which they're totally different, bringing their own light to the world in ways that we have no input or control over.

Kingston's breathing evened out to a soft, gentle little snore. I laid him down and climbed in beside him. I'd never liked the little room we were in. My uncle Gary, who was also a drug addict, who also had AIDS, died in that room—in that very bed—twenty years before. I'm pretty sure my grandmother had changed the mattress by then, of course. But not much else had changed. The room had always felt heavy to me, a little dark. But with Kingston around, there was a shift in the energy. It was subtle, but noticeable, at least for me. Much to my surprise, I fell quickly and thankfully to sleep.

The next morning we were up with the chickens. Even though my body clock had somewhat adjusted to East Coast time I still considered 8:00 a.m. to be 5:00 a.m.; it was the energetic equivalent of getting up at dawn.

Papa kept trying to make me eat something while Grammy fed the baby. Kingston was so proud of his two little teeth and he loved to use them. It tickled my grandmother to give him little bits of toast slathered in butter and watch him go, "Yummmm!" My brother and grandfather were dragging our bags back outside to the trunk of the car, arguing the whole way about what should go in first and what should go in last. Those two, born on same day, were practically the same person, one in an old body and one in a young body. Therefore, they could never agree on anything.

My sister's oldest two children, Naiyah and Chris, were in school. But the twins were still home. Each one grabbed a leg and started climbing up my body, all the while pleading, "Please don't go, Auntie! Please don't go! We want to play with Kingston!"

I didn't want to stay, but it sure would've been nice to be able to take them with me. I covered their little faces with kisses and promised to be back soon, even though I knew that it probably wasn't true. My father showed up in time to kiss us and wave good-bye. I was grateful and I didn't cry, even though I was pretty sure it was the last time I would see him alive.

By the time Kingston and I finally pulled out of the driveway, we were way behind schedule. I had friends and cousins along the route that I'd promised to see. Now there would be no time. Too frazzled to have planned properly and embarrassed to call, I just ignored my broken promise and figured I'd make it up later after we were back in Los Angeles. There was only one person I'd still have time to see, and even that was now debatable. We'd really have to fly down I-95, wobbly car seat and all. And, of course, it was raining again. Kingston loved the rain. It hardly ever rains in Los Angeles. So for him, the rain was not a nuisance or a vehicle liability. It was an event. He loved the sound that the rain made as it pounded on the car roof. He cooed and giggled and try to match the noise of the plinks and plops.

"Pa, pa, pa, pa! Ba, ba, boom!" he sang as we drove down Marlton Turnpike.

I turned off I-95 to I-295, praying that we didn't get lost out in Maryland. I wasn't used to this route, but I'd promised to meet my friend Rodney for tea and it was the only promise that I actually intended to keep. We were supposed to meet at a Starbucks somewhere close to the airport just over the state border. Every five minutes I glanced at the clock on the dashboard. Our plane was leaving at four o'clock. So we needed to be in the airport by 2:30 or 3:00 at the absolute latest. And I had to leave enough time to return the car to Avis, check in, and make it to our gate. It was already 1:00. Part of me wanted to just call Rodney and tell him I couldn't make it. But I refused. I just trusted that we'd make it.

So much had happened in the past few days. I told myself that I deserved a brief respite, some time to sit and laugh with someone whom I really appreciated. I didn't need much. Just a few minutes to remember myself. I wanted to reminisce about a time when I wasn't somebody's mom or wife or chauffeur, to sit down and laugh like I was that person again. So off to Starbucks we went.

We pulled into the parking lot at ten minutes past one. I got the baby out of his car seat (apologizing to him profusely for rushing and being so rough) and ran inside. After all that, Rodney was nowhere to be found. If the baby hadn't been sitting in my arms, I would've cussed like a real New Yorker. Instead, I ordered a chai latte and sat down by the window to wait. About fifteen minutes later, Rodney walked through the door.

Oh look, I thought in my snarkiest inside voice, *there's Roddy the Hottie.* He made it after all.

I never called my ex-boyfriend Rodney by his nickname, "Roddy the Hottie," to his face. He would've revolted. He was a tall, handsome, Yale-educated, professional-tennis-playing, mountain-climbing entrepreneur who studied neuroscience in his spare time. The nickname was so far beneath him that he refused to respond the few times I said it out loud. He simply turned his nose up and looked away.

So Rodney was late and *still* had no sense of humor, I decided. But I had to admit I was happy to see him. Rushed and frazzled, but happy.

"Kuwana," he said, hugging me. "How are you?"

"I'm wonderful," I replied. "It's so good to see you."

Our hug lasted for a good long while before he turned to the baby and said, "This must be Kingston. Look at him. He's beautiful. You must be so proud."

"I am," I gushed. "He's such a blessing. I never could've imagined how much one little person can completely alter your entire life."

Kingston smiled and gurgled, pulling at Rodney's overcoat.

"I'm going to go get a tea," he said. "I'll be right back."

I checked the time on my phone as he walked toward the back of the barista's line. Well, I had about fifteen minutes left, twenty at the most. We'd have to make the best of it. Rodney slowly edged up toward the front of the line. With each step he took, my good feelings about seeing him again faded. Something was off. His shoulders were stooped, his eyes darting nervously from one direction to the next. I held the baby little bit closer.

"Sorry I took so long," he said as he returned to our little table. "Someone was following me."

"Who?" I asked, instantly concerned.

"*They* are."

"Who is they?"

"They're the ones with the sundial."

He lowered his voice and looked around again. "They followed me here because they want the information that I have in my brain. I was hoping you could help me get it out. I need to hide it before they come back."

Kingston reached out to Rodney and I gently pulled him back, looking around casually. It was the middle of the day. There were some other people in the coffee shop, but not many.

"So tell me, Rodney, what's been going on lately?"

Rodney sighed. "You might as well know. I haven't been feeling very well lately. I gave up my business a while ago. I've been having run-ins with these people who have been following me."

"Do you see these people now?" I asked.

"No, they're not here now. But they'll be back soon," he said ominously. "And before you say it, no, I'm not crazy. I know it sounds crazy, but it's not. That's the problem. I can't get anyone else to believe me when I say that I've been seeing these people and they've been downloading this incredible information into my brain about light therapies to heal people of cancer and death and about cell and limb regeneration and even astral travel. I wish I could convince someone this is all real. But not even my mother believes me. She thinks I need to go on meds. What do you think?"

Talk about awkward.

"I think your mother has your best interest at heart," I said tactfully. "I think she loves you very, very much. More than you could ever know. So maybe you should take her advice. It's possible that she can see things that you can't see right now. It might be in your best interest to trust her vision."

The baby reached out again, and as casually as possible, I pulled him back again. Every second I sat in that seat with the cold chai tea in front of me, my heart broke a little bit more. I had a plane to catch.

"Hey," Rodney said. "If you wait out front, I'll drive around and you can follow me. I'll put you on the right road to the airport. It's a shortcut. You'll make it in twenty minutes, in plenty of time for your flight."

As he smiled at me, he looked exactly like the person I knew years ago. So when I smiled back, it was genuine. Maybe that's what our best friends and soul mates do for us. Maybe the greatest contribution a friend can make is to see us as we truly are, no matter what presents itself in the moment or what the circumstance. Having authentic connection means having people who can see our souls peeking out from beneath the mental and emotional garbage that sometimes drifts over our truth.

True to his word, twenty minutes later I was turning off toward the airport exit. We returned the rental car and I made a mad dash from the shuttle to the ticket counter, with

> Maybe the greatest contribution a friend can make is to see us as we truly are, no matter what presents itself in the moment or what the circumstance.

the baby strapped to my chest, car seat in one hand and lugging three bags behind me. I rushed up to the desk only to be told that they couldn't find my reservation. I'd have to step to the side and wait while they figured it out.

That's what I got for stopping at Starbucks.

By this time I was sweating and practically sick to my stomach with worry that we were going to miss our flight. I'd been so excited to come home, come east—so desperate to see the people and the places I loved and missed so dearly. But now, after all these weeks and lots of soul-searching, there was nothing I wanted more than to get my ass on a plane and go home—to my real, current home.

I wasn't going to find what I'd been looking for in any place, no matter how dear to me. I wasn't going to find it in any other person. Everyone (as I was plainly being reminded) had their own issues to deal with. I'd wanted a touchstone, a quiet place, the ability to be grounded in my space. Kingston had that in me. I was the expression of his connection to his source, which was rock solid, unquestioned, and unshakable. But the root of that peace and connection lay within him. Therefore, I reasoned, my touchstone must also lie within me. The people and the places that I'd sought out, that I believed were mine, were really the outpicturing of my connection to

> I started wondering what would happen if I could disconnect my judgments about my life, stop coloring all my stories with meanings that may or may not have any truth to them.

the truth within me, which was unmovable.

Something unexpected tends to happen when tremendous life changes take place, like becoming a mother or losing those we love. For the first time, I took a deep breath and silently acknowledged being lost. I acknowledged being overwhelmed. I acknowledged feeling ill-equipped and lonely, even though I was never, ever alone anymore. I acknowledged being angry with the people I loved for not pulling through life and winning in the ways I wanted them to. I acknowledged the fear that I wasn't living the life that I wanted to either, so, really, who was I to judge them? I acknowledged desperately wanting a break from it all and knowing that I wasn't going to get one. At least not anytime soon.

Then a funny thing happened. Instead of feeling worse as I thought about all the things that were going on, I began to feel a measure of acceptance. And centeredness. And then, finally, peace. I was still sweating and waiting and overburdened and late. But in the midst of all that, I was also quietly learning how to disconnect from the need to make these conditions wrong. They were simply conditions, indicators that life was moving me forward in the ways that it needed to. No more, no less.

I started wondering what would happen if I could disconnect my judgments about my life, stop coloring all my stories with meanings that may or may not have any truth to them. Kingston, still strapped into his carrier, was busy enjoying the sights and sounds and smells of the airport. He judged none of it, of course, because he was a baby and hadn't learned how to assign value judgments to otherwise neutral things. To be able to do that was an adult accomplishment.

In reality there was nowhere I had to get to, literally or metaphorically. There was nothing wrong with where I was. Accepting the moment exactly as it is inspires the perfection and beauty of that moment to reveal itself. So life wasn't trying to overwhelm or punish me. It was looking to come through me, just as Kingston had come through me—not to be controlled but to be given the opportunity to experience and to play. It was my job to connect willingly to what was showing up as my life, my experiences, and then to keep moving forward, to extend that bridge far beyond my present reach.

If I could do that, and make my plane, then I might be in business.

Making Time: Kingston and the Lost Art of Putzing

The opposite of play is not work. It's depression.

—BRIAN SUTTON-SMITH

KINGSTON AND I SNAGGED THE LAST SEAT ON THE PLANE, all the way in the back row. Thank you, United. As soon as the PLEASE FASTEN YOUR SEAT BELT light blinked off, Kingston crawled into the lap of the teenage girl sitting next to us and started talking. He was always chatting up older women.

"Oh, what a sweet baby," said the flight attendant, leaning over my shoulder. Kingston smiled at her and held up his arms. The woman was smitten.

"May I hold him?"

"Sure," I said, handing the baby over.

"Hello," the woman in the blue uniform cooed. "What a beautiful little boy you are!"

The other flight attendants must've heard them talking, because suddenly Kingston was enveloped in a little circle of smiling faces.

"Do you want to come back and see where we work?"

The flight attendant looked at me and I nodded that it was OK. With that, they all disappeared into the back of the plane with the baby. *Well*, I thought, *it's not like they can go anywhere.*

I took the quiet time as a reprieve to meditate just a little bit. My mind was usually full of random thoughts, all skittish and unwieldy, like wrestling kittens except not nearly as cute. I tried to organize my thoughts just a little, to see and acknowledge them before letting them pass.

So many things were coming to an end. At the same time an entirely new phase of life had begun, whether I felt ready for it or not. I recalled once talking to Rev. Michael about beginnings and endings. I made mention of the idea of the circle of life. He corrected me by saying that, outside of *The Lion King*, there's no such thing as a circle of life. Rather, life is more like a spiral. The trajectory of your spiral at any given moment depends largely on the kinds of choices you make and how you respond to the contrasts that life offers. Life isn't a circle—circling would indicate that life always stays on the same level, like a hamster on a treadmill. That's never the case, even when it feels as though that's exactly what we're experiencing.

Life is dynamic, ever evolving, moving forward even when we don't want to move with it. Eventually, we must graduate from kindergarten to the first grade. And eventually, first grade also comes to an end. We spiral up. The tests get harder. When the tests get complicated it's easy to become caught up in the idea of doing more, faster, just to maintain. But that's never the way to keep moving forward.

> Life is dynamic, ever evolving, moving forward even when we don't want to move with it.

You leave too many important things undone or unnoticed in your wake.

I was about to walk back into a whirlwind. I could let it suck me up or propel me forward. The choice would be mine.

Once the plane landed, I strapped the baby into his carrier against my chest. The flight attendants blew kisses to Kingston and waved good-bye. They pinned a tiny little pair of wings to the front of his carrier while he laughed and clapped ecstatically. I smiled at how happy the smallest things could make him. And he always had time to make a new friend. Kingston was like a toothless little yogi, lost in wonder of *what is* in any given moment. Isn't that the magic of babies? And isn't that the quintessential dilemma of adults? We're always running here, running there, thinking ahead. In the adult world, thinking ahead makes us rational and responsible. You're congratulated when you relinquish the art of being lost in the moment.

The problem is that fulfillment and joy can only be had now. Self-acceptance can only be had now. Contentment can only be had by looking at the world as it is and finding what you see pleasing. Compassion can only be had by looking at the world and seeing the things that are not pleasing through the eyes of love and surrender. When we live primarily for the future, life becomes more difficult because there are too many unknowns to fear. When we live in the past, we tend to create too many meanings out of too little information and a haze of cloudy memories. Blame and wishful thinking fog over our ability to claim the prizes of experience that have made us who we are. Any way you look at it, it's crazy making. We get lost in our thoughts about life rather than being immersed in the wonder of life itself. That makes for a lot of busywork and confusion.

Cory met us at the baggage carousel. Together, we lugged all our belongings out to the parking lot. Kingston did most of the talking on the way home. He gurgled and squealed and cooed all the way up La Cienega Boulevard. Only when we pulled into our driveway and Cory was heaving our many bags out of the trunk did I finally ask, "So, what do we do now?"

He turned to face me. "We find somewhere to live. Fast."

We had exactly twenty-two days to find a new home. That wasn't a lot of time under the best of circumstances.

We came up with a plan: Cory and I would pick out likely prospects in the evening, and Kingston and I would drive around to visit them during the daytime. Meanwhile, it was time to start packing. You never know how much stuff you actually have until you have to put it all in boxes. As we got down to work, I realized that packing up to move is a decidedly different activity when you have a seven-and-a-half-month-old baby who wants to pack with you. It seemed like everything I tried to do took three times as long as it should have, at least according to the timekeeper in my mind. I felt like I was falling behind, like everyone else was arriving early and getting down to the business of life before I even had a chance to get out of the parking lot. Everything was a rush.

Unfortunately, Kingston and I saw the situation from two different vantage points. Where I saw urgency, he saw new opportunities to play and explore. If I made a 10:00 a.m. appointment to go see a new house, at 9:35 a.m. he would dump a bowl of cereal over his head, requiring hair washing and an outfit change. If I had our clothes freshly changed and our bags packed, ready to head out the door by 9:50 a.m., at 9:51 a.m. there would be an unmistakable odor of decay wafting from his diaper and a happy smile on his face. I could never catch up.

In the evenings, when I wanted to start packing boxes and folding clothes, the baby would decide to lend a helping hand. That meant he either wanted to be in my arms or in a box, playing peekaboo. Either way, he was intent on lending his exuberant personality to the effort (no need to say thank you). There was no time for my freelance clients, much less my book. I was in constant motion from the time I woke up in the morning until I crawled into bed late, late at night. There was always one more thing waiting to be done. I almost felt guilty about going to sleep if I hadn't checked off enough boxes on the mental to-do list.

It was proving very difficult to find a place suitable for all of us in the part of the city where we wanted to live. Some places were absolutely gorgeous but well out of our price range. Other places were within our price range but left too much to be desired in other areas. Which is a nice way of

saying we saw a whole lot of dumps. In some places, I refused
to even get out of the car and go inside. Every day that passed
without a credible lead left
me feeling more and more
desperate. I would look at my
son, whether he was laughing, sleeping, playing, or crying, and feel the weight of my
responsibility for him draped
over my shoulders.

> Somewhere inside,
> I still believed that there
> was a tremendous bless-
> ing waiting to be recog-
> nized and embraced
> in the other side of
> all this mess.

It was my job to make sure that he was safe and secure.
There could be no excuses. Things had to be done. And the
only way I knew how to get them done was to put my nose
to the grindstone. Cory and I hustled day and night. As the
days passed, determination began to give way to anxiety. I
felt disconnected from the home that we lived in, but there
was no indication that something new or better was about
to manifest in its place. It would've been so comfortable and
easy to slip back into old patterns of not seeing the brilliance
and abundance all around us, only what we didn't have and
what wasn't showing up.

At that point, I would've given anything to be on the
hamster wheel. Damn the spiral. At least a hamster wheel is
stable. In the bigger picture, of course, the problem wasn't
the circumstances. The problem was my perception of the
circumstances, which turned my spiral into a whirlpool with
a wicked undertow. Somewhere inside, I still believed that

there was a tremendous blessing waiting to be recognized and embraced on the other side of all this mess. But my fear, and the resulting busyness, simply stopped me from seeing it. And the end of the month was rapidly approaching.

The second-to-last Saturday of the month also happened to be the birthday party of the son of one of Cory's closest friends. Weeks before, Cory had told them that we'd come to the party. We'd been so caught up in our unfolding housing drama that we'd never canceled.

"Maybe that's a good thing," Cory said. "Let's go. Aragorn's party should be fun. Let's take the afternoon off and go have a good time with the baby. We deserve it."

I wasn't convinced.

"The best way to do this is divide and conquer," he continued. "I'll go to Toys 'R' Us to get the present. You get the baby ready. We'll meet back up here and head to the Valley."

The baby looked at me expectantly.

"Dada? Dada?" he chirped.

"No, Mama," I answered. "Dada is the guy who's escaping down the driveway as we speak."

"I heard that," Cory yelled.

"Good, I'm glad," I yelled back as the door swung shut behind him.

I carried the baby's plastic bathtub to the front of the house and filled it with warm water in the kitchen. Then I undressed him in front of our herb garden window and sat him down in the water. He squealed and splashed and kicked, grinning up at me with his two-toothed smile. Within minutes, the counter-top, the front of my shirt, and the floor in front of the sink were all soaked. He had a mountain of soapy hair standing up in little tendrils all over his head and a little soap beard from where he'd tried to eat his bath water. All I could think was how I'd have to change my clothes and mop the kitchen floor before we could leave. Great.

I washed the soap from Kingston's head, dried him off, and put some sweet-smelling baby lotion all over him. With a prodigious effort, I managed to stuff all his squirming body parts into a cute little lion cub outfit. Then I went back to tackle the floor and the counter and clean the toys out of his tub. Only when all that was finished did I remember that I needed something to wear too. And I had to decide fast because we were already late. Frustrated, I snatched something from the closet and hoped it matched. Cory wasn't back yet, so I had just enough time to feed the baby. He was bound to get hungry on the trip out to the Valley.

We had a little spaghetti left over, which the baby loved. I heated it up and put it in his bowl. Then I fastened the baby's bib around his neck and strapped him into his high chair. Just as I was about to give him his first bite, the phone beeped. Figuring that Cory was probably texting me, I walked over to the coffee table to check. When I walked back to the table, approximately eight seconds later, Kingston had ripped the bib from around his neck, grabbed his bowl off the table, and poured the entire contents over his head.

He smiled at me and then made his mouth open really wide, imitating my look of horror. Cory walked through the door a few minutes later to find a half-naked, cackling baby seated on the dining room floor in a puddle of chunky marinara sauce.

"What happened? I thought you were going to get him ready."

Cory eyed me suspiciously, as though I was responsible for the mess, like I'd just decided to fling some tomato sauce across the room for the hell of it. It was all I could do to not leap over the dirty baby and strangle him with a fistful of capellini noodles.

By the time we got out of the house and made it all the way out to Tarzana, the birthday party was halfway over. Having no concept of time, Kingston stayed blissfully unaware of anything except that he was ready to have fun. The bright colors and the balloons and the music and the pizza smell and the excited children running around in superhero costumes delighted him in every way. I tried my best to stay angry and flustered, but it was hard. There was too much joy going around.

Little by little, I relaxed. Sitting at a corner table, I watched Kingston crawl around on the floor with one of the other babies, an adorable little girl named Clarke. He was slow and she was fast. He hadn't completely got the hang of the whole crawling thing, but he was determined to keep up. The discovery of his body, the symmetry of his arms and legs, and his newfound ability to maneuver across the carpet filled him with such obvious wonder. The entire purpose of his life was to play, to discover.

I was open to that principle. I believed in the idea that we've all been born into this world to be the arms and legs that God uses for exploring. In fact, our species has evolved not through its strength and will alone, but through its poetry and dreams. What was my baby if not a perfect line of poetry, delightfully unfolding, moment by moment, through the grace of God? In my rush to be productive, I had forgotten that the very things I most wanted to produce were already here in front of me—joy, play, laughter, love, and all these things in great abundance.

I didn't want to create a world where I was constantly chasing things. It's a losing proposition no matter how you look at it. Because the more stuff you catch, the more you're inclined to believe that you've tracked down your good by the strength of your own cunning and the sweat of your brow alone. But the constant pursuit, the need to grab and hold on to things, is the very foil that allows life to slip away. I knew that—but merely knowing something doesn't count for much. You can know about wisdom and still not be wise. Wisdom, like all the other qualities of the spirit, manifests only when you live what you know, when you consent to be a doer of the word and not just a hearer only.

I pretended to be paying attention as I talked to the people around me. But all the while I was praying for an anchor that would hold me to a deeper place of understanding long enough for me to catch its meaning. I no longer wanted to grab on to things, like a house or more money; I wanted a vision. I wanted to hold my hand open to a new vision of my life, and myself, as already perfect, whole, and complete. What exactly did that look like?

Later that night, Cory drove back out to the Valley to his parents' house, leaving us at home to get ready for bed. There was a lot to do and it was already late in the evening. I still had to clean up the day's adventure with spaghetti, not to mention give the baby yet another bath. This time the birthday cake was to blame. He wasn't allowed to eat any of it yet, but he had absolutely no problem snatching and wearing it.

My mind was on the cleanup and bathing, the brushing and wiping, the hunt for new diapers and clean clothes. Kingston tugged on my ears and my cheek as I carried him through the house, trying to accomplish each of these tasks one-handed. Almost against its own will, my mind had already drifted somewhere into the afternoon of the next day, wondering what to fix for lunch and what the baby would wear after we got home from church. We'd have to do a quick change before heading back out again to shop for food and meet with Lisa and the kids.

Right in the midst of my mental gymnastics, my back went out. Or, more accurately, I felt two ribs on my left side gently pop out of place. I knew exactly what the feeling was because it had happened to me when I was pregnant. And I knew what to expect. I counted down in my mind: *five, four, three, two, one...*

The most excruciating pain lit up the entire left side of my torso. It felt like someone jabbing a dull knife repeatedly into my left lung. I leaned against the wall in the living room and slid down, holding the baby in front of me. I couldn't walk or move. Kingston waited for a second. Then he bopped me in the nose. *Get up! Get up! Let's go!* But I couldn't go anywhere. Instead, I sat on the floor being pummeled by the baby and wondering when would be the earliest I could get an appointment with our chiropractor.

I also couldn't help but consider the mechanics of answered prayer. Not five hours before, I'd prayed for an anchor to hold me in a place of focused awareness.

Clearly, this wasn't what I had in mind.

However, I had to admit that I was at a complete standstill. And, boy, was I focused. It appeared to be as good a time as any to stop, breathe, examine, and reconsider my penchant for constant motion. So I allowed myself to just relax and be still. As still as I could be with a feisty baby climbing on top of my head.

With Kingston draped over my head like a hat, I took the opportunity to remind myself that this wasn't a bad thing; stillness is a necessary part of growth, balance, and equilibrium. Granted, I'd envisioned the experience of stillness as something more along the lines of a weekend meditation class, but this time I was willing to take what I got. Setting the intention to experience stillness meant agreeing to release the things that I had to do, my thoughts about those things, and anxiety masquerading as responsibility.

As we waited for Cory to come home, I began to sit with the idea of balance as a pathway toward inspiration and fulfillment. Sometimes balance looks like taking the time for a deep and grounding meditation. And some-

> Setting the intention to experience stillness meant agreeing to release the things that I had to do, my thoughts about those things, and anxiety masquerading as responsibility.

times, when you're stubborn, you have to learn about balance while a baby sticks his foot up your nose and climbs to the top of your head. Either way, it is always a necessary and timely lesson.

Love Is Like Musk— It Attracts Attention

Being deeply loved by someone gives you strength, while loving someone deeply gives you courage.

—LAO TZU

I have found the paradox that if you love until it hurts, there can be no more hurt, only more love.

—MOTHER TERESA

WE NEVER FOUND A PLACE TO LIVE. THE MONTH ENDED AS it began, with us searching. With just three days left, I sat in the middle of our living room surveying the sea of boxes stacked all around me, shoved into every corner and stacked onto every tabletop. Where would they all go? The new owner was about to take possession of the house, so there was no going back. As much as I tried not to think the thought, the one word that kept popping into my mind and flashing in bright neon colors was *homeless*. The landlord had lost the house and now we were about to become homeless.

Of course, I was being dramatic. We were never going to be out on the street, set outdoors like empty milk bottles. (Did I mention that our midcentury bungalow even had an adorable bottle slot built into the laundry room wall where, back in the day, the milkman would leave bottles of fresh, sweet milk? There was even a space to store the empties. Very *Honeymooners*. Very cute. Not ours. Not anymore.) We had too much family, both our real family and our family by desire, to ever be in danger of living on the street. But the reality was that our home was gone.

As the baby crawled through the cardboard obstacle course, I had visions of meeting our landlord in a dark alley.

I *hated* our landlord. When it came to our landlord, I felt anything but spiritual—unless you counted me saying

> Children are emotional seismic detectors.

that he better pray if he ever met me in that dark alley. Just as I was getting worked up in my mind again I heard a thump and leapt to my feet, searching for that slippery baby in the mountains of cardboard. He had fallen on his bottom behind a large box of books.

"Mama?" he chirped.

He had been trying to eat the box. I could tell from the slobber trails all along the sides. I picked him up and nuzzled him.

"Come here, little man. Mama's sorry. I'm not paying attention. Lost in thought, I guess. But that's not your fault."

Kingston gurgled in agreement and gently boxed my nose. All was forgiven. The closeness of his warm body and the smell of milk on his breath was like a sedative for my nerves. I instantly relaxed, my heart expanding to meet his. This was a conscious act, to raise my energy to match my baby rather than staying down where I was. Children are emotional seismic detectors. When we're fretful or angry or in pain, they respond. Many times the behaviors that drive us the most crazy are simply the child's way of mirroring back what we adults have been feeding him through our exchange of energy. I didn't want to do that.

A few months ago I probably would have been unaware

of those opportunities to do better, to shift. But now I was aware. I recognized the call within me to stay focused and grateful for the circumstances that life was offering up to us right now. Because, ultimately, everything was working out for the best. In this way, my concept of surrender deepened. It stretched me and grounded me in the moment. Learning how to surrender was about learning how to grow my root system so that I could go deeper and higher at the same time. That was my job. Everyone has a job, and mine was to make sure that the roots in our family went deep. My spiritual assignment was to become the very thing that I'd been looking for my entire life. It was time for me to surrender and know my place.

Surrender and gratitude are spiritual qualities that are birthed in the heart of motherhood, when no one else is looking. They shape your experience, the things that you see and don't see along the path. I thought about what Rev. Michael had said a million times: surrender is your willingness to release something of a lower nature to make room for something of a higher nature to enter your life.

I breathed Kingston in, aware of each breath as an act of surrender, a willingness to believe that even in this moment my highest good was being served and brought forth. Something beautiful was being born in the midst of change that could never have been manifested any other way. After all, self-love and appreciation come before manifestation, not the other way around. In other words, I had to be at peace in the midst of the storm, rather than expecting peace to come to me later, after the storm had passed.

Recognizing these things helped. But that didn't stop the challenges from appearing, or even slow them down. When we finally admitted to ourselves that we'd have to move in with Cory's parents for the time being, I felt like I was living the synopsis of a seventies sitcom: *With nowhere else to go, they appeared at the home of Cory's parents. Several days earlier Cory and Kuwana's landlord had thrown them out, requesting that They. Never. Return.*

It was hideous, on the face of it. We were *those guys*, the boomerang kids, returning home with children and pets and a whole house full of furniture in tow. Sure, the same thing (and worse) was happening to people all around us and all over the country. It was the apex of the Great Recession. But that didn't change my feelings about it. I watched my judgments carefully, trying not to get sucked in by them.

Moving day came. I was saved by the fact that I had to take care of the baby. Cory and his friend Charles took care of all the heavy lifting while I tended to Kingston, so I didn't have to see all my worldly possessions get shoved onto a moving truck. We still didn't know what to do with half of our furniture. There'd be no room for it at Cory's parents' house, so it couldn't go on the truck.

Just as we were wondering out loud what to do with it all, Xiomara pulled up curbside, behind the moving truck. I'd barely seen my friend since the baby shower. She was always so busy. Xiomara was a maven. She knew everyone, every-where. You couldn't throw a stick in any city where black people congregated without hitting someone who knew Xio. When you needed something done Xio would appear, quite like a Panamanian Mary Poppins, making calls, contacting people, and getting things done. She wasn't necessarily around when you wanted her. But to her credit, she was always there when you needed her.

"What are you going to do with all this furniture," she asked, striding through the open front door into the living room, swooping the baby up in one hand and holding her cell phone against her ear with the other. She was on hold on a totally different matter, so this was a good chance to talk.

"I don't know," I said. "But we have to figure it out soon. Now."

"Let's get rid of the bulky stuff. You can always buy new furniture when you move. Everything else can be stored in your in-laws' garage."

I blinked. Sounded simple enough to me.

"OK. But how do we get rid of it? We're supposed to be wrapping this whole move up in the next three hours."

"Leave that to me," Xio said. As she spoke, she'd already clicked off her other call and was busy uploading ads to Craigslist from her cell phone.

"Just let me know how much you want to sell these things for."

"Don't sell anything. Just give it all away."

"You sure?" Xio raised an eyebrow at me. Then she laughed. "Of course you are."

By the time Cory and Charles finished loading the truck, the couches, coffee tables, and the office furniture from the guesthouse were all gone. There was nothing left.

It was time to go. We were starting fresh.

I waited for the depression to descend as I stood at our front door for the last time. It didn't happen. Instead of feeling myself wobble and creak under the weight of self-recrimination, I actually felt a little bit lighter.

I was getting free.

What an interesting process. It looked nothing like what one would assume. I had so many ideas in my head about what purpose and fulfillment and freedom of expression should look like. I was beginning to see that I had everything ass-backward. I'd been programmed to check boxes off a list: loving husband, check; perfect, healthy son, check; nice car, check; good credit, check; inspired career, check (well, working on it, anyway); beautiful home, check. Sort of. When you start getting into the middle ground, the gray "sort of" areas, it's very easy to become unsettled and confused if all you have to work from is a checklist. You become boxed in by all your boxes, whether checked or not. But there was so much more to life than that.

Kingston and I hugged Xio good-bye and followed the moving truck to Cory's parents' house all the way out in the Valley. Willie and Elaine had recently divorced, though they'd agreed to share the family home. There were reminders everywhere of the family's thirty-plus years in that house and of Willie's fifty-five years traveling the world as an entertainer. Willie was a pioneering ventriloquist and an accomplished singer. I remember being four years old, sitting on my grandfather's knee, watching "Willie Tyler and Lester" perform with Flip Wilson on television. Somewhere, on the other side of the country, my future husband, who was six months older, was doing the same thing. Who knew?

There were pictures all over the wall in the den of Willy and Lester with some of the greatest legends in entertainment of the last half-century: Lena Horne, Dolly Parton, Sammy Davis, Jr., Michael Jackson. Willie knew them all. Even George and Weezie Jefferson. There were pictures of Cory everywhere from all the television shows and films that he'd acted in. There were portraits and magazine covers of the whole family displayed proudly on the walls. There were even pictures of Cory from his boy band days displayed not quite so proudly out in the garage (where they belonged). The Tylers had a real sense of history in that house. Now, somehow, we needed to blend our new family with all that had come before.

We didn't know how long we were going to be there, so we'd agreed to make the best of the situation. We'd put a bid in on a new house but we hadn't heard yet whether or not it was accepted. There was no way to tell what our timeline might look like. This question mattered a great deal to me. It didn't seem to matter as much to Cory or to Kingston.

Especially Kingston. Truth be told, as soon as we stepped foot into his grandparents' house, he was in soul heaven. He had instantaneously manifested an unlimited supply of love and affection.

I watched him roll around on the living room floor, babbling and yelling, "Uh-oh!" every time he pulled something down. Then he'd smile happily up at me before reaching out for something else to upend. He was eight months old and, true to form, he was beginning to talk already. I could never be one of those parents who complained about not being able to understand their baby. If nothing else, Kingston could get his point across. He seemed to thoroughly enjoy the challenge and the art of communication. And now he had just doubled the number of people he had to talk with. I marveled at him, noticing how he still thrived despite his parents' seeming misfortune.

But as soon as I had the thought, I realized that Kingston wasn't thriving despite misfortune (mine or anyone else's). He was thriving precisely because *he saw no misfortune*. He appeared to approach every situation from the vantage point of curiosity and inclusion. What does this situation have to offer me? What do I have to offer it? It was the law of reciprocity in action. He gave his all to every interaction, without judgment and without expectation. So it was easy for him to elicit feelings of love and generosity in other people. The fact that he had super-fat cheeks and big doe eyes with the longest eyelashes ever also didn't hurt.

Sans cheeks and eyelashes, I would have to work with principle. In order to experience truth and joy and unconditional love in my life, I had to give those qualities first,

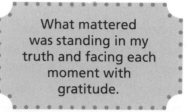

What mattered was standing in my truth and facing each moment with gratitude.

starting with myself. I had to court them, challenge myself to recognize them everywhere I looked. Only then would these qualities begin to consistently show up as the situations and circumstances of my life. It could never be the other way around.

It didn't matter whether I finished my book or not. (Ultimately, I didn't. I started this one instead.) It didn't matter whether I made lots of money and had lots of prestige or not. It didn't even matter whether we found a beautiful new home or not. What mattered was standing in my truth and facing each moment with gratitude. Because in every moment, in every breath, was an opportunity to be replenished and reborn, to stay connected to life's flow.

Over the next few days we got settled in as best we could. Cory and I scoured the real estate sites every night after the baby fell asleep, plotting, planning, and scheming. It was almost as much work as actually moving and unpacking. By the weekend, we needed to recharge. Agape was having its annual Revelation Conference. Cory had to attend and I was happy to tag along. It was a welcome break from our unending real estate machinations.

That year, the conference was held in Burbank. Colorfully dressed people with high vibrations and blossoming awarenesses descended on the Burbank Hilton in droves. Kingston was in his element. He clutched my neck and squealed at each new sight, smell, and sound, his roly-poly legs pumping excitement. There was singing and dancing and theatrical performances and lectures and yoga and art exhibits, all crammed into three days. By Saturday morning, I was pooped. I needed a break from my break.

Elaine had come with us, and while she waited in line for a back adjustment from the hugging chiropractor we decided to rest for a few minutes. Kingston and I plopped

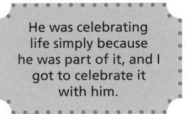

He was celebrating life simply because he was part of it, and I got to celebrate it with him.

down in a lobby chair just in front of a set of glass doors and the adjacent elevator. Every time either set of doors opened, people would stop to talk to the baby. Kingston obliged every single one of them. He reached out to the strangers as if they were family, smiling, cooing, squealing, playing coy when necessary.

Within minutes, a crowd had formed around us. Kingston held court like a pro. He was the star and I was his backup performer. My job was to prop him up, then give him space to do his thing. The crowd loved him.

In the midst of the laughter and the lightheartedness, a woman walked off the elevator alone, her eyes downcast, her short blonde hair hanging into her face. She stuck out from the crowd like a mourner in the middle of a circus parade. Kingston saw her first. I didn't notice her at all until he began gesturing in her direction. She looked up at us at the same time. As soon as Kingston caught her eye, he started clapping, as if he'd been waiting for her to arrive. Everyone else looked back at her, smiling approval and laughing.

The woman seemed taken aback. I smiled and asked, "Doesn't it feel wonderful to be applauded everywhere you go?"

Her face absolutely lit up.

"Yes," she said. "Yes, it does!"

She beamed and everyone beamed back, caught up on a wave of unattached joy.

By nature, I am a proud mama. But I had never been prouder of my son than I was in that moment. He was celebrating life simply because he was part of it, and I got to celebrate it with him. How often do we forget, or refuse, to celebrate ourselves exactly where we are, the way we are? How often do we see an imperfect try as a failure rather than another step closer to success, resisting the perfection in our imperfections?

The people around us were all still laughing. I laughed too, but for different reasons. I laughed to acknowledge the journey that I was on, knowing that motherhood, like every other part of life, was about embodying the timeless qualities of our being as completely as we can in this human form.

We'd come so much further than I had realized. Our journey together had carried me deep into the territory of answered prayer without my even knowing it. Laughing in gratitude, I recalled having prayed to know the nature of my purpose on this planet. Finally, I found it: to be love.

About the Author

KUWANA HAULSEY is the author of the critically acclaimed novels *The Red Moon* (Villard) and *Angel of Harlem* (One World/Ballantine).

As a 2007 Penn/Faulkner Foundation honoree, Kuwana was named one of three New Voices in American Literature. That year, *Angel of Harlem* was chosen as one of the New York Public Library's Books for the Teen Age. The Blackboard Bestsellers organization awarded *Angel of Harlem* the Medal of Courage, a prize created specifically to honor the book.

The Red Moon was chosen as a *Washington Post* Notable Book of the Year. It also won a finalist prize at the Hurston-Wright Legacy Awards.

In addition to writing novels, Kuwana is an editor and freelance journalist. She has written features and cover stories for publications such as the *Washington Post, Ebony* magazine, the New Jersey *Star-Ledger*, *Uptown* magazine, and *Odyssey Couleur* magazine.

An editor of the biography *Hal Jackson: The House That Jack Built*, Kuwana was part of the team that brought the legendary story of broadcast pioneer Hal Jackson to life. Published by HarperCollins, the book is exhibited at the Smithsonian Institute.

Kuwana lives in Los Angeles with her husband and two sons.

Photograph by Cory Tyler.

TO OUR READERS

Viva Editions publishes books that inform, enlighten, and entertain. We do our best to bring you, the reader, quality books that celebrate life, inspire the mind, revive the spirit, and enhance lives all around. Our authors are practical visionaries: people who offer deep wisdom in a hopeful and helpful manner. Viva was launched with an attitude of growth and we want to spread our joy and offer our support and advice where we can to help you live the Viva way: vivaciously!

We're grateful for all our readers and want to keep bringing you books for inspired living. We invite you to write to us with your comments and suggestions, and what you'd like to see more of. You can also sign up for our online newsletter to learn about new titles, author events, and special offers.

Viva Editions
2246 Sixth St.
Berkeley, CA 94710
www.vivaeditions.com
(800) 780-2279
Follow us on Twitter @vivaeditions
Friend/fan us on Facebook